▶ **Live To Your Local Cinema**

DOI: 10.1057/9781137288691

Other Palgrave Pivot titles

G. Douglas Atkins: **T.S. Eliot Materialized: Literal Meaning and Embodied Truth**

Michael Bennett: **Narrating the Past through Theatre: Four Crucial Texts**

Arthur Asa Berger: **Media, Myth, and Society**

Hamid Dabashi: **Being a Muslim in the World**

David Elliott: **Fukushima: Impacts and Implications**

Milton J. Esman: **The Emerging American Garrison State**

Kelly Forrest: **Moments, Attachment and Formations of Selfhood: Dancing with Now**

Steve Fuller: **Preparing for Life in Humanity 2.0**

Ioannis N. Grigoriadis: **Instilling Religion in Greek and Turkish Nationalism: A "Sacred Synthesis"**

Jonathan Hart: **Textual Imitation: Making and Seeing in Literature**

Akira Iriye: **Global and Transnational History: The Past, Present, and Future**

Mikael Klintman: **Citizen-Consumers and Evolutionary Theory: Reducing Environmental Harm through Our Social Motivation**

Helen Jefferson Lenskyj: **Gender Politics and the Olympic Industry**

Christos Lynteris: **The Spirit of Selflessness in Maoist China: Socialist Medicine and the New Man**

Ekpen James Omonbude: **Cross-border Oil and Gas Pipelines and the Role of the Transit Country: Economics, Challenges, and Solutions**

William F. Pinar: **Curriculum Studies in the United States: Present Circumstances, Intellectual Histories**

Henry Rosemont, Jr.: **A Reader's Companion to the Confucian** *Analects*

Kazuhiko Togo (*editor*): **Japan and Reconciliation in Post-war Asia: The Murayama Statement and Its Implications**

Joel Wainwright: **Geopiracy: Oaxaca, Militant Empiricism, and Geographical Thought**

Kath Woodward: **Sporting Times**

DOI: 10.1057/9781137288691

palgrave▸pivot

Live To Your Local Cinema: The Remarkable Rise of Livecasting

Martin Barker

University of East Anglia, UK

palgrave
macmillan

DOI: 10.1057/9781137288691

First published 2013 by
PALGRAVE MACMILLAN

Palgrave Macmillan in the UK is an imprint of Macmillan Publishers Limited,
registered in England, company number 785998, of Houndmills, Basingstoke,
Hampshire RG21 6XS.

Palgrave Macmillan in the US is a division of St Martin's Press LLC,
175 Fifth Avenue, New York, NY 10010.

Palgrave Macmillan is the global academic imprint of the above companies
and has companies and representatives throughout the world.

Palgrave® and Macmillan® are registered trademarks in the United States,
the United Kingdom, Europe and other countries.

ISBN: 978–1–137–28870–7 EPUB
ISBN: 978–1–137–28869–1 PDF
ISBN: 978–1–137–28868–4 Hardback

A catalogue record for this book is available from the British Library.

A catalog record for this book is available from the Library of Congress.

www.palgrave.com/pivot

DOI: 10.1057/9781137288691

Contents

List of Illustrations

Tables

Figures

DOI: 10.1057/9781137288691

Acknowledgements

I first became interested in the phenomenon of livecasts after attending an NT Live presentation in Aberystwyth in 2009. Loving the show (*Phèdre*), I was intrigued by the hesitations I and friends sensed among the audience about how they could take part. Should they dress up as if going to the theatre? How should they respond to seeing the audience at the source-event? What would it mean to laugh, when the actors couldn't hear? How should they use the interval, when there was no programme? Was it OK to clap at the end – was it worth doing so? Long fascinated by the challenges of researching audiences, I began to devise a project, and ultimately – after a pilot in Aberystwyth – approached a number of the companies associated with livecasting to ask whether they would be interested. I would do the work for free, asking help only in publicising a web questionnaire. Eventually, one company – Picturehouse Cinemas, which owns more than 20 cinemas and provides the transmissions to many others – took up my proposal, and the research took place in 2009. I only subsequently realised that among the reasons others might have backed away was that they were already doing their own research. Indeed, the more I looked, the more I realised that this phenomenon had ramifications far beyond my initial interest in the audience. Like Topsy, this research kept on growing. I like that. I tried out my first thoughts and results in a number of conference presentations. Some acute critical feedback helped me refine what I felt I could confidently say. I now offer this book as a 'come-on' to other researchers who have skills and knowledges that could throw a whole new light on this phenomenon.

DOI: 10.1057/9781137288691

This book has been greatly aided by helpful responses from a wide range of people who often didn't know me at all, from a variety of places and fields of work. I believe that I have thanked them all individually, but I hope, more importantly, that if they read this they will all feel that I have made fair use of their ideas, even where (sometimes) I have not agreed with them. I owe especial thanks to three people: Gareth Bailey, Cinema Manager at Aberystwyth Arts Centre, who has unstintingly responded to my queries and requests; Alastair Oatey at Picturehouse Cinemas, who took the chance of enabling me to carry out my audience research, when he could not be sure what benefits there might be; and Paul McDonald of Nottingham University, who chucked a tough yorker of a question at me when I presented a half-formed version of this book's central ideas. I'm delighted, finally, to be a part of the launch of Palgrave Pivot initiative, and my thanks go to Felicity Plester for making my journey to here smooth and pleasant.

DOI: 10.1057/9781137288691

1

Introduction: The Success Story with No Name

Abstract: *Introducing the phenomenon of 'livecasting', this chapter recalls its history, and the range of contributory forces which shaped its emergence. Originally known only under its industry name, 'Alternative Content', the idea of beaming live performance events into cinemas had been conceived some years earlier, but primarily as a means of promoting the sale of expensive new digital projection systems. The first successful events were in 2006, when the New York Metropolitan Opera, driven by difficult financial circumstances, took things in an unexpected direction. The surprise success of these events led other arts organisations to develop the format, and to begin to create institutional infrastructures for these events. But the issue of a public 'name' for them remains unsettled.*

Barker, Martin. *Live To Your Local Cinema: The Remarkable Rise of Livecasting*. Basingstoke: Palgrave Macmillan, 2013. DOI: 10.1057/9781137288691.

On the last weekend of 2006, the New York Metropolitan Opera launched a new initiative. Captured by up to a dozen high-definition digital cameras in front of more than 3,000 attendees, a live performance of Mozart's *The Magic Flute* was beamed to 100 digitally equipped cinemas in the USA, the UK, Canada, Norway – and, with a delay, Japan. This followed close on a slightly earlier glitzy experiment in which Puccini's *Madame Butterfly* was relayed to screens in Lincoln Center Plaza and Times Square to an assembled crowd which included many New York celebrities. *The Magic Flute* – itself to be the subject of a further experiment in March 2007, when a performance was audio-streamed to the internet – was the first of an experimental run of six beamed performances, which also included Bellini's *I Puritani*, the world premiere of Tan Dun's *The First Emperor*, Tchaikovsky's *Eugene Onegin*, and Rossini's *The Barber of Seville*, and was the first and most visible sign of a new phenomenon which was to grow and expand at a breathtaking pace. Variously known as 'simulcasts', 'cinema livecasts', 'beamed live perform-ances', they were and are known to the cultural industries that spawned them simply as 'Alternative Content'. To one of the few small pieces of academic writing about it that I have to date located, they constitute 'digital broadcast cinema' (Heyer, 2008). This book tells the story of their emer-gence, and explores their impact and significance.

This phenomenon, which spans theatre, opera and ballet perform-ances, various kinds of concert and some prestige sports events, has not yet received any significant academic attention. Yet it surely deserves it. It is being seen, as I will shortly show, as among the leading-edge devel-opments encouraging the digitisation of cinemas. Box office takings from these events are attractive in at least three ways. They are attracting back to cinemas audiences who had largely deserted them. They com-mand a higher ticket price – with the bonus that many people book for whole seasons at one go. And they are, in the main, sell-out successes. In the words of a 2012 Picturehouse Cinemas promotional advert, this is nothing less than 'transforming your cinema'. They also pose a series of challenges to many traditional theories in fields such as cinema studies, theatre and performance studies, and television studies.

How did they come about? The brain-child of the NY Met's new General Manager Peter Gelb (who had joined the company from Sony), these broadcasts were the response to worrying times at the opera house. Ticket sales for its huge 3,800-seat theatre had fallen to below 75 per cent. Traditional sponsorship sources were drying up (in 2006 the Met had to be rescued by a $25-million personal donation from Mercedes Bass, wife

DOI: 10.1057/9781137288691

of Texan oil tycoon Sid Bass). The average age of its audiences had reached 65. Gelb's challenge was to 'attract a younger, more hip, audience to opera ... the intellectually curious arts consumer, people in their 30s or 40s who, for example, like art-house cinema' (UPI, 2007a). This was a tricky manoeuvre, Gelb being quoted variously as not wanting to 'dumb down' performances, but aiming to put opera 'back in the mainstream' (UPI, 2007b). The events certainly proved attractive. American carriers reported 91 per cent capacity audiences, seven UK cinemas sold out, and Canada's reached 75 per cent. The $17.95 charge – considerably above normal cinema prices – compared very well with prices at the Met itself, where tickets could cost up to $350. And for this you got a close-up 'front-of-house feel'.

The turn to digital cinema

But this was about much more than just opera. Here was a development which had been brewing for six years, with ideas, technologies, companies spinning off at a perilous rate.[1] The launch date was 2000, when the first viable digital cinema camera was announced. Initially limited to pre-screen advertising, its potential to address several of cinema's fundamental troubles nonetheless looked enormous. Print costs had topped $1,800 per unit. Digital unit costs could be as low as $300 (Merritt, 2004). In one presentation, David Hancock from *Screen Digest* estimated the studios' potential savings at an annual $2 billion. Meanwhile, falling audiences in many countries found cinemas struggling, and this not long after a boom in cinema building. Digitally equipping cinemas could expand the repertoire, and – if non-traditional materials could be found – lead to the mecca of higher unit prices.[2] In the six years up to the Met's launch, a veritable cauldron of ideas was stirred – not least the development of a complex business model known as the 'Virtual Print Fund' (a mechanism for managing the costs of digital installation, but which has been argued to suit commercial cinemas taking films close to their release, and to disadvantage cinemas showing specialist films to minority audiences). 'Alternative Content' became a watchword – but entirely, for now, among interested business and industry insiders, who were multiplying greedily:

> At last month's ShoWest, the annual industry showcase in Las Vegas, conventioneers got a taste of the Super Bowl in 3-D, according to Brad Brown, president of the marketing company Brown Entertainment Group. 'It's the

DOI: 10.1057/9781137288691

Wild West for alternative-media sources', he says. 'Nothing is unexpected anymore'. (Galupo, 2007)

But the initial ideas had little to do with things like opera. It was to the Super Bowl, the Tour de France, international football and pop concerts, that is, mass sports-and-entertainment spectacle, that providers expected to turn – although other early enthusiasts included Fox Faith, who saw the medium as a means to distribute religious films. Experiments included *Jekyll & Hyde: The Musical* transmitted to an invited audience in Los Angeles to demonstrate Boeing's satellite system, which caused a stir when it drew repeat audiences (Canadian Corporate Newswire, 2001), and a Morrissey concert in six US cities (PR Newswire, 2005). Other early ideas included showing rave films on nightclub screens. But before anything could go beyond this experimental stage, there had to be agreement within the industry on technological standards and protocols. The launch of digital audio in the 1990s had seen too many competing systems, and the studios were determined not to allow this to be repeated. So everything stayed pretty much in-house until 2005, when the cross-studio Digital Cinema Initiatives, with input from the Society of Motion Picture and Television Engineers and the American Society of Cinematographers, delivered a huge report detailing proposed technical specifications (Digital Cinema Initiatives, 2005).

This overcame the first hurdle. Now producers needed something to persuade cinema owners, who were often distinctly reluctant to invest in the technology (Forde, 2002b).[3] The prospect of 3D film was one key component in the persuasion package (along with the general advocacy of individual figures such as George Lucas, who had hoped that his Spring 2002 digital release of *Star Wars: Attack of the Clones* would kickstart cinemas' uptake). Digitisation would enable the introduction of 3D, which would in turn allow cinema, at least briefly, to outstrip television (another re-run, surely, of the introductions of colour, widescreen, Dolby sound and so on). Also, sophisticated encryption systems could reduce risks of piracy. Early developments were focused on digital's general cinematic possibilities, with *Collateral* (Michael Mann, 2004) being among the earliest films to test the market. The first digital projector (the Christie CP2000X) debuted in 2005, but was marketed so aggressively that the studios backed away. The first film really to demonstrate the potential to be gained from 3D was *Chicken Little* (Mark Dindal, 2005), which grossed $300 million worldwide. Even more to the point, 'Digital

DOI: 10.1057/9781137288691

cinema was in its early days, and there were only a limited number of screens but in the end those screens, which represented about 15 percent of the total number, generated almost 85 percent of the revenue' (Digital Cinema Report, 2011). This was good, but not enough. 'Alternative Content' became a device to persuade investors to bite the digital bullet.

Just occasionally, individual countries had for their own reasons begun the digital change-over – notably the UK, where the Digital Screen Network was created by the UK Film Council as a component in its strategy for promoting British films. This network enabled many small, independent, mainly art-house-oriented cinemas to install digital projectors. This of course then affected the whole early ecology of digital uptake and where its benefits could go (in small towns, commercial cinemas could become jealous of the head-start arts cinemas had gained when 3D arrived). And it perfectly suited the shift which then took place to offering high-culture Alternative Content.

Theatre-cinema, and other experiments

Cinema owners and managers had good reason to be cautious of the optimistic promises about digitisation, and not just because of the natural caution of those running knife-edge businesses. For those who knew them, the historical precedents did not bode well. There was a long tradition of attempts to link live theatre with television, some mainly forgotten. Louise Anderson (2010) has drawn attention to perhaps the earliest of these attempts, 'Scophony'. Before World War II, and the hiatus this imposed on television, there had been experimental demonstrations of the possibility of planting TV's small images on big screens. Anderson tells Scophony's brief story as the first video relay system designed to present TV images on cinema screens. There was an initial demonstration in July 1930 at the London Coliseum, but the first practical trial was on 23 February 1939 at the Monseigneur News Cinema, Marble Arch. Both because of the War and because of Scophony's inherent weaknesses, no more came of it. More widely remembered is 1950s theatre-cinema. Douglas Gomery (1985), its pre-eminent historian, tells of the studios' attempts to reincorporate television into their operations, having been foiled in their attempts to buy the companies. Contrary to standard histories which have suggested that the studios ignored the rise of television, Gomery shows how acutely aware the studio bosses were of the challenge to their businesses. In the context of fast-falling cinema attendances, theatre-cinema attempted to sell the idea

DOI: 10.1057/9781137288691

of showing sporting events and television dramas on large screens. A great deal of research went into the enabling technologies: 'The major Hollywood corporations played an active part in this phase of innovation with their own experiments, demonstrations, and corporate maneuvers. For example, Warner Bros., in May 1948, presented its own version of RCA's system to 3,000 invited guests at the Burbank studio' (1985: 57). Notably this led, says Gomery, to a phase of experimental cooperation between the studios. By 1952, 102 cinemas had been equipped with their expensive kit.[4]

Peter Krämer (1996), drawing on Gomery's research, argues that the studios, far from ignoring television, foresaw the inevitability of its rise, but their early attempts to manage its challenge were thwarted by anti-monopoly pressures. He also makes a case that among the studio owners were some, notably Sam Goldwyn, who foresaw that this would shift their business model to one in which more independent producers would develop projects – which of course became increasingly the model between the 1950s and 1970s. As companies adjusted to the fast-shifting conditions after World War II, theatre-television was tried out. These were transmissions to large screens of events such as major political speeches and sporting events. For the studios, the attraction was not just potentially boosting audiences, but, as Krämer argues, establishing that television could be a public, large-screen medium. However, high installation and transmission costs, Federal Communications Commission challenges and relatively low audience take-up meant that within a few years the experiment was abandoned. With these precedents, then, the vibes were not positive, even if the context was different.

But the NY Met, on a roll, was determined to build on its lead position.[5] Its second and subsequent seasons increased the number of broadcasts, with eight livecast productions in 2007–8 attracting 920,000 people, and generating gross income of $13 million in the USA (with a further $5 million from abroad). This pushed other opera companies to try to get a share of the spoils. Sydney Opera House, the UK's Royal Opera House and Glyndebourne, Gran Teatre del Liceu (Barcelona) and Teatro Real (Madrid) all eventually mounted livecasts, with varying degrees of success. The Met responded by imposing restrictions on cinemas taking others' work during their own season.

A widely reported 2002 Cinema Expo International seminar among distributors and exhibitors ('Beyond Digital Cinema: Alternative Content and New Revenue Sources') brought many of the issues into focus. 'Alternative Content' was no longer an option; it was a necessity.

DOI: 10.1057/9781137288691

The issues were simply how, and how soon. What was badly needed was reliable research on audience interests, to guide decisions. Wendy Aylsworth from Warner Bros. reported intriguingly on one experimental screening of an NBA playoff game:

> 'Those people gathered to watch the event, and not the quality, because the game was out of town and they wanted to watch it with other Lakers fans,' Aylsworth said. (Kemp, 2002)

But that possible community of watchers could pose problems. Discussing the prospects of showing football via the new technology at the Berlin International Film Festival, Dave Monk (Texas Instruments) declared: 'Soccer is huge in Europe, so it seems a natural for alternative content. But we have to figure out how people react to a venue that's not a normal venue for soccer. We have to ask: "What do people think about watching soccer in a place where they sit down rather than stand up, where they don't have bars and can't mill around in quite the same way?"' (Donahue, 2003). This combination of bullish confidence and hesitancy is key to understanding the ways Alternative Content developed. It also helps explain why, following the NY Met's success, a flurry of business reports emerged trying to model its future.

In the UK the first big player to join the parade in a determined way was the National Theatre, through a spin-off arm, NT Live.[6] Drawing on the Met's experience, in 2009 their first beamed event, *Phèdre*, judiciously starred the popular cinema and television star Helen Mirren. There followed Shakespeare's *All's Well That Ends Well*, a Terry Pratchett adaptation, *Nation*, Alan Bennett's *The Habit of Art*, and the bawdy *London Assurance*, which alone reached audiences of 150,000 people in 22 countries. Its second season included Danny Boyle's *Frankenstein*, with an innovative experiment of two livecasts in which its stars, Benedict Cumberbatch and Jonny Lee Miller, switched lead roles. Other art-forms sought entry. In November 2009 the Paris Opera Ballet was transmitted across the world, including to 30 UK cinemas.[7]

Smelling success

By 2009, Alternative Content had made its way beyond the business pages, becoming news wherever one looked. It was undeniably doing good business. *Screen Digest*, in the first overall business report, stated

DOI: 10.1057/9781137288691

that global takings would soon top \$500 million, adding that 'Cinema is fast becoming a multi-arts venue'. Its projections were striking:

> The market for alternative content has progressed from one that was almost entirely experimental and ad hoc, to one now in early market evolution. The steady growth of the digital screen base to over 12,000 globally had provided sufficient scale to experiment with new content offerings in cinemas, and to secure longer term and more original content arrangements. The arrival of films such as *Avatar* pushed a second wave of cinema changeovers – with predictions that by 2013 over 80 per cent of British cinemas will have gone digital (with, of course, some resultant pegging back of the independents as their fringe advantage is undercut). Globally, the market for alternative content was worth \$45.7m in 2008, equivalent to 0.4 per cent of gross global box office revenues. This is expected at least to double to hit \$104.6m in 2009. Moreover, the entire alternative content market will be worth \$526.5m by 2014. (Jones and Hancock, 2009)

If correct, this would be a staggering growth rate, taking Alternative Content to 5 per cent of the global box office within eight years of its birth. But then prospects seemed to stumble. In 2011, *Screen Digest* reported again, putting a figure of \$112 million on its 2010 value, 'a growth of 51.7% over 2009', and reporting that of 37,000 cinema screens at the end of 2010, 22,000 were equipped for 3D (Hancock, 2011). But although cinema seat occupancy was still as low as 25–30 per cent globally, Alternative Content (which had been expected to raise this significantly) remained a 'very small proportion of overall cinema revenues'. Opera remained top favourite, with theatre and ballet entering the scene significantly. So, although the market was still growing, the bullishness which had shown in *Screen Digest*'s first report is markedly absent. And around the same time, Melissa Keeping (2012) for Digital Cinema Report noted that one of the UK's early promoters, Arts Alliance Media, had unexpectedly cut back on staff: 'sources close to AAM say that all indications so far point to the division's high overheads. While its output of alternative content was impressive, with Pearl Jam, Chasing Legends, Iron Maiden's Flight 666 and most recently George Harrison's Living in the Material World biopic among its hits, the box office results were evidently not substantial enough to sustain the business long term.'[8] Keeping suggests that NT Live might not be the company finding it has overreached itself. His conclusions are interesting:

> On the plus side, the alternative content industry has never been so buoyant, and this news should not be taken as indicative of the industry as a whole. The cinema-going public is becoming more savvy and particular as time

DOI: 10.1057/9781137288691

progresses, raising the bar for distributors who can no longer offer poorly produced alternative content, which has happened on occasion in the past, and raising expectations as a whole. Content providers are now much more aware of the potential profit in a theatrical release and are beginning to build this into their schedules alongside a world tour and a new album, something which even two years ago was a rarity. With operators now choosing to specialise in one or two content areas rather than offer a bit of everything, the market is beginning to demarcate itself into a premiership of several larger key players and a first division of smaller boutique agencies. In time it's possible that the smaller companies will be swallowed up into the main competitors, bringing with them the niche experience and the key contacts that make this business what it is, and the industry may begin to resemble the mainstream studio business, though without the monolithic infrastructure and gargantuan budgets. (Keeping, 2012)

The implications in this, that audiences are becoming more discriminating and demanding, should be remembered as we move to considering Alternative Content's cultural and aesthetic aspects.

Seemingly from nowhere, then, this development launched into a public sphere that, at least at first, appeared to take it up enthusiastically. Spin-off companies blossomed, along with new alliances. Some governments got quite excited, welcoming it not only for its digital super-modernity, but also (as we will see) for its promise of uplifting cultural goals (European Union, n.d.). The first failures were being considered and lessons learnt. Alternative Content looks to be a fine work in progress, a new, exciting, sustainable feature of our cultural landscape, even if its strength, spread and implications are still not entirely clear. And it certainly raises a number of fascinating broader questions. In the remainder of this book, I consider five in particular:

1   What are the emergent aesthetics of these performances? How like or unlike films are these screened performances? How are their producers managing the balance between the home audience – who remain vital, not least for authenticating performances' liveness, by being seen and heard – and the much larger distributed cinema audience? What bonus extras are offered to cinema audiences to keep them coming?
2   Who are the audience? What do we know, so far, about them (their age, sex, class, locality, expertise, etc.), and about their responses to the performances? How are they learning to judge the effectiveness of this new way of receiving culture?

DOI: 10.1057/9781137288691

3   How in particular are they dealing with one feature of
    Alternative Content: its not-quite-liveness? What indeed is at
    stake here, in the meaning and significance of 'liveness'? We will
    see, in fact, that this concept has been the topic of a series of
    quite disparate debates in a range of fields. But all the resulting
    very different theories are inevitably put at risk by Alternative
    Content, which unapologetically refuses demarcations. Where
    might we go, then, for a useful model to think about this new
    kind of 'near-liveness'?

4   What is all this doing for the *status* of art-forms and cultural
    practices? The past thirty years have seen extensive debates about
    the nature and operation of hierarchies of value around cultural
    forms and traditions, not least following the work of Pierre
    Bourdieu. How does Alternative Content alter things here?

5   Finally, what research needs to be done next? What *don't* we know or
    understand about Alternative Content? I hope that I have managed
    to speak intelligently about quite a range of issues. But there are
    definitely others (for instance, relating to law and to business
    modelling) where I simply lack the necessary grounding and
    competence. Yet I can see a range of serious emerging questions.

Closing this introductory chapter, I want to return to that question of
names. Names are significant, because they can be more than mere
labels. Where there is an agreed name for a phenomenon, meanings
and expectations can sediment around it. In a related field, film scholar
Rick Altman (1999) has shown how film genre names have frequently
been acquired through the turning of adjectives into nouns: 'musical',
'western' and 'action' – the last one interesting because of the double
move (from noun to adjective and back to noun again) involved. His
point is that in formative moments, detaching adjectives from their
accompanying nouns (*musical* drama, comedy, thriller, etc.) indicated
that 'everyone now knew' what to expect – and indeed might be becoming a bit wearied by it. In previous cases of technological developments
offering new experiences, their names shouted their claimed benefits:
Widescreen, Technicolor, Surround Sound, 3D. A name can do more
than group and point; it can sum up experiences and make promises.
The fact is that 'Alternative Content' has no resonant public name, only
a rather roundabout 'what it isn't' industry label. I believe this relates to
still-unsettled questions about these events' cultural status.

DOI: 10.1057/9781137288691

Nevertheless, I have chosen henceforth to refer to these events as 'livecasts', because it is short, and sort of descriptive. Official, public christenings must wait.

Notes

1   The Met *does* in fact have 'previous' with respect to transmitting its performances. As early as 1948 ABC Television filmed the opening night of *Otello*. Technically rather naïve (there were real problems with lighting for early cameras, and synchronisation of action and camerawork was reportedly poor), it did well enough that opening nights were transmitted for the next two years, until cost considerations killed the experiment (see Citron, 2000: 43–50). Met performances were again relayed, to TV sets in the late 1970s, under the title 'Live From The Met', under seasoned television directors such as Kirk Browning. But again early excitement was not sustained. An interesting essay by Richard Kirkley (1990) explores a related history for Canadian television's experiments with Electronic Theatre.

2   Hancock's presentation also demonstrated the greater income per head from 3D, because of the higher attendant prices.

3   ' "116 digital screens out of 130,000 does not constitute a commercial roll-out," said National Association of Theatre Owners (NATO) head John Fithian at the annual Cinema Expo exhibitors' conference in Amsterdam this week. "We are still in a testing phase" ' (Forde, 2002b).

4   Intriguingly, some of those involved in developing Alternative Content were keen to draw upon the work of academics such as Gomery. The European Digital Cinema Forum borrowed from his and others' historical work in their 'The EDCF Guide to Alternative Content in Cinemas' (n.d.).

5   In America, regional opera houses were also soon expressing nervousness about threats to their own audiences.

6   I am grateful to this book's anonymous referee for pointing out that in 2009, a year before NT Live's launch, the UK's Royal Opera House screened *Don Giovanni*. But certainly NT Live's large-scale thrust gained far more public attention.

7   A good idea of the range of kinds of event now digitally flowing to cinema screens can be garnered from a visit to the Digital Cinema Report website: http://www.digitalcinemareport.com/taxonomy/term/20?page=4.

8   There have certainly been misjudgements. Although I have not been able to obtain figures, insiders have told me, for instance, that the beaming of Jamie Cullum's Cheltenham Festival performance flopped badly, probably because Cullum does not have a strong following among jazz aficionados.

DOI: 10.1057/9781137288691

2

The Aesthetics of Livecasting

Abstract: *This chapter looks closely at a number of specific livecasts (theatre and opera) to reveal their construction and aesthetic properties. It examines the ways in which four theatrical events from the National Theatre, London, work hard to construct an experience which will be like that of spectators at the event (as opposed to a filmed production), but simultaneously offer cinema audiences bonus features (including 'bravura moments') giving a kind of privileged insight. This shifts the focus from the overall stage to particular moments and exchanges between characters. Opera performances – with their heightened artificiality – have required a rather different approach, in which the use of the overall stage remains of greater importance. Three New York Met broadcast operas are closely analysed to show emerging solutions to these challenges.*

Barker, Martin. *Live To Your Local Cinema: The Remarkable Rise of Livecasting.* Basingstoke: Palgrave Macmillan, 2013. DOI: 10.1057/9781137288691.

DOI: 10.1057/9781137288691

What can we say about the visual and aural management of livecasts? What styles, what aesthetic sensibilities are put on offer to audiences? What, indeed, is the 'performance' that the cinema audiences get to watch? My account draws on notes taken after attending three livecasts in 2009–10 (*Phèdre*, *All's Well That Ends Well*, and *The Kitchen*), and on closer examination of five other livecasts from 2011 (*King Lear* and *Frankenstein* from the National Theatre, and *Lucia di Lammermoor*, *Don Pasquale*, and *Anna Bolena* from the New York Met). I intend no judgements on the quality, success, or effectiveness of any of these (although I have my personal preferences). Instead, I aim simply to characterise how vision and sound were constructed for each of the livecasts.

Typically, surrounding a livecast performance are adverts and trailers for upcoming events, scene-setting introductions by some recognisable figure, and shots of the assembling audience. Introductions are part informational (an opera's plot, the history of a play, or cast members' previous experience), and part promotional (say, the work that has gone into design and production). Sometimes, as we will see with *King Lear*, the way this is done can make significant promises. But the rest, and especially perhaps the audience shots, are also important for the 'guarantee' they provide of the event's simultaneity. Here are people finding their seats, talking, then hushing as the lights go down. Their responses (laughter, clapping) are overheard. Occasional shots will register at least the front rows. Here, surely, is proof of liveness.

There is a first level, then, driven by the limits and compromises imposed by the need to protect the source-event and the experience of the physically present (let's call them the house) audience:

1   Cameras must not obtrude for the present audience. No doubt this required some experimentation as to what worked and also what was acceptable to the house audience.[1] However, livecasts are important enough that for the performance at which they are filmed, seats are removed to make space for cameras, and (with the National Theatre) a track for one mobile camera is installed.

2   For the same reason, dialogue has largely been shown by means of two-shots, as against over-the-shoulder shot and reverse (the norm for much film and television).

3   Camera locations tend for the same reasons to produce a combination of low-angle shots (as from the sides of the auditorium or the orchestra pit) and eye-level shots (as from

DOI: 10.1057/9781137288691

the sides of the stage), with occasional high-angle additions from an eagle's-eye camera. Sometimes these high-angle shots themselves provide a special kind of aesthetic experience. Highly choreographed movements whose interrelations may hardly be visible to those attending the event can become visible through well-chosen high shots, emphasising cinema audiences' privileged access.

4   Sound-capture is usually by means of approximately balanced mikes attached to actors (throat and head mikes seem to predominate), with some additional capture of ambient audience responses.

5   For this very reason, there can be small uncontrollable drops in sound-capture as a result of characters turning their head away from their own mike's ideal position or entering 'dead' areas.[2]

6   Stage lighting produces non-naturalistic depth for the cameras, with the result that characters can seem to be 'pooled' by light, and stage and sets drop out of vision. Especially when this effect combines with semi-close-up shots which put other parts of the stage out of the focus, characters can seem pulled forward in a way that is unlikely to be reproduced for the house audience.

7   Generally, there is a predominance of un-cleaned sound, so that any non-diegetic music or sound carries the timbre of its whole-theatre source. But at what volume, and with what sense of proximity, this is captured will vary considerably.

Once they have accommodated these general constraints, screen directors can follow some very different strategies.

Creating a theatre aesthetic

Take *King Lear* (NT Live) with Derek Jacobi as a case in point. The first livecast filmed at the small Donmar Warehouse, it was introduced by a series of interviews with actors and directors talking about the specialness of the space. This is, we are firmly told, a special theatre, with 'no bad seats'. 'We enjoy being this close to the audience' – whose knees might almost intrude onto the apron. One actor recalls being stopped by a woman who pointed to a spot of paint on her coat and told him – seemingly without complaint – that this had landed on her during a performance of *Red*. If

DOI: 10.1057/9781137288691

cinema audiences register and remember these claims, they will surely expect to feel close to the action. Yet these are the very qualities which, I could argue, they did *not* get from the presentation. *Lear* had a plain set, with floor, walls and ceilings clad simply in wooden planks, to give (so cinema audiences were advised in advance) a primitive 'pagan' feel. Matching this, camerawork and sound-treatment were also unadorned. Under the direction of Robin Lough (a seasoned TV director whose experience includes the Proms), cameras were used throughout to keep a strong reference to the overall stage. Sometimes this produced a strange formality. For example, Lear's confrontation with Goneril was captured mainly by a wide shot, from a slight angle, that caught actors isolated at four or five different stage-points. These wide shots aside, the main forms of camerawork were two-shots, occasional near close-ups, and travelling shots following a speaking actor. Actors never spoke to camera. Edgar, making his defining 'Now gods, stand up for bastards' speech, addressed various parts of the audience, including those in the balcony, but spoke past the camera.

In the entire production there were only three what I call 'bravura moments'. One was strongly motivated by the production design. Lear, on the 'blasted heath', delivers 'Blow, winds, and crack your cheeks'. The scene opened with the stage lit as if by lightning, seen through the cracks in the cladding, with loud wind noises. As Lear, centre-stage, breathes in, all other sound is cut, and he whispers the first part of his speech, miked to produce a slight echo. Spot-lit, he was captured (better: observed) by a high camera, towards (but never into) which he often looked. The second bravura moment came at the play's end. With the dead Lear held in Kent's arms, camerawork composed a two-shot of them like a painting of the dead Christ in a saint's arms – and then slow-dissolved to a high shot of the entire stage held stock-still. Across the dissolve, muted sounds of birdsong hinted for a moment at the wider natural world. The third such moment was less pronounced, but struck me forcefully. The blinded Gloucester stands alone back-stage under a 'tree' as the crucial battle takes place through sound only. The camera capturing him swung across and simultaneously pulled back, emphasising his isolation, but also hinting at a swirling disorientation.

These exceptional shots aside, most of the filming comprised static or slow-moving, long-held shots, with undemonstrative cuts between. Because in the main lighting was also plain (with just sweeping rig changes to indicate changes of location), only occasionally did

DOI: 10.1057/9781137288691

camerawork interact with lighting to produce its own effects. On just one occasion – when Kent is imprisoned in the stocks, and Edgar uses front-of-stage to deliver a monologue – the cameras' heightened contrast effectively blanked back-of-stage to seal off the two phases of action.

Soundscapes were simple throughout. With Lear's heath speech the sole exception, all voices were simply live-captured, at stage volumes. Openings of scenes had occasional sound-effects, with – again – a feel that these were captured off-stage, rather than transmission-controlled. But these were few and far between, and functioned with lighting as scene-changers. Audience responses (occasional laughs, for instance) were muted and 'behind'.

If I had to sum this up, I would say that throughout there was an inescapable sense that we are *watching a stage*. We are observing actors performing – but never especially for us. We are never so close or so involved that the special proximity the Donmar offers is reproduced for us. It needed the rhetorics of the opening interviews for us to know about the qualities of this space. For cinema audiences to 'get' this, they have to be willing and able to treat the camerawork as entirely *transparent*, unobtrusive, and invisible in itself. They must be able to reproduce 'being there' in their heads.

Compare this with *Frankenstein*. This powerful National Theatre production, in which Jonny Lee Miller and Benedict Cumberbatch alternated roles between performances as Frankenstein and Monster, was directed by Danny Boyle, who has both theatrical and film experience. Tim van Someren (its Director for Screen) and Christopher Bretnall (Technical Producer) are both leading figures in filming large external broadcasts such as live concerts. This time, there were from the outset many ways in which the production's screen design signalled clear extras for its cinema audiences. The performance opens with a single toll of a bell. For the theatre audience, this might as well have been a recorded sound, given that there was no prior indication, and the bell was not especially visible. For cinema audiences, it was conveyed by an upwards close-up shot onto the bell. The shot is repeated near the end, when the bell tolls to mourn for Frankenstein's little brother William.

This performance was captured by multiple cameras, including one high-level swooping, one directly overhead, several (including one mobile) front-of-stage and two appearing to shoot from the sides of the auditorium. Overall, shooting was predominantly lightly mobile two-shots, tracking the interactions of pairs of actors. Just occasionally these

DOI: 10.1057/9781137288691

were accented with brief close-ups. Camera movement remained slow and unobtrusive, with most shots long held. Cuts tended to be shifts of angle on a two-shot, supplemented with shot reminders of the overall stage-set. A small degree of predictiveness was evident, as when a character's arrival might be signalled by a camera pickup. For instance, near the end, a cut took us to an off-stage camera, just before the Creature arrived through the audience. The overhead camera was used sparingly, for especial emphasis – for instance, catching in near close-up the Creature's upturned face reacting to snow, then later watching in a more distant shot his rape of Elizabeth.

But always there remained an acute sense of front-of-stage. On a number of occasions, characters turned to the 'front' to utter key lines or show reactions. Always, they looked past camera at 'the audience'.[3] Most notably this happened when Frankenstein and the Creature, in momentary alliance, deliver bitter lines towards the audience about 'little people leading little lives'. The audience too became visible several times: at opening and close of the play, of course, but also when characters used the apron's margins.

Lighting was often strongly expressionist (the Creature's opening long, stylised 'birth' scene, for instance, pulsated with reds and oranges). At other times, it was very zoned, allowing easy transfer between stage-separated elements of action (particularly during the scenes in which the Creature is befriended by an old blind musician – seen in a house – unbeknownst to the two younger people who are 'farming fields' on the stage edge). Camera sensitivity surely accentuated this, making the off-scene elements almost invisible for cinema audiences (unlikely to be so clearly demarcated for the house audience). Sound seemed hardly manipulated. Audience reactions were reduced, as if coming from behind the cameras. With no evident throat mikes, it was hard to tell whether there was any managed balancing of voices with sound-effects or overlaid music (of which the production had a considerable amount).

There were cinematic flourishes, between scenes, often from a wide shot through slow dissolve to black, to the next scene introduced by a long fade (the only dissolves in the entire production) up into a new lighting set. There were also particular bravura moments. Early in the play, a steampunk vehicle parades across the apron, carrying an array of characters, two of whom then provide the Creature's first interactions with people. Its arrival was captured by canted shots and close-ups which accentuated the peculiar vehicle and its crew's outlandish dress.[4] Yet in

DOI: 10.1057/9781137288691

the other direction, in farm scenes, no attempt was made to avoid the stagey artificiality of having the Creature entering back-stage unnoticed by two talking characters.

The main consistent features of these two plays overall, then, appeared to be these. Two-shots constituted a kind of standard mode, but some mobility between angles for these, plus a small amount of camera movement, minimised the sense of static observation. Front-of-stage was sacrosanct. The cameras never claimed for themselves the moments when actors crossed the 'fourth wall' and spoke out to the audience – they *observed* that happening. But here, there were clear bonuses for cinema audiences. Featured elements could be treated more cinematically, as could transitions. And moments of especial drama could be picked out with those emphatic high and overhead angles.

What is evident from both these plays is the importance of well-judged selection of moments of extreme stage-actorliness. Monologues, moments of intense physical embodiment, vital duologues: all are up for accentuation – with perhaps the test being not to choose too many, lest the force of 'close-ups' be diminished. (I put 'close-ups' in quote marks to signal that, of course, stage gestures and movements almost inevitably remain larger and broader than would seem appropriate for cinema or television – thus a close-up for a livecast will almost always include torso and arms. Extreme close-ups are unknown here.)

A brief contrast with the National Theatre's 2011 production of *One Man, Two Guv'nors* is illustrative here. This broad comedy piece stars James Corden as the servant continuously caught between two stools. The production plays heavily on its localisation, in several senses. Before the performance, we see not only the theatre audience assembling but another audience outside, on the piazza, being entertained by 'period' dancing as they prepare to watch the play on a large external screen. Within the play, there are period jokes (1963: 'I predict, in twenty years, there will be a woman in Downing Street...'), historical references (for example, to the burning of Brighton Pier) and house markers (audience members being brought on stage – including one who is soaked with a fire extinguisher, whose status as 'plant' is revealed only at the end, when she joins the curtain-call). The most distinguishing feature of this production is that the theatre audience's sound is raised to match stage levels, to ensure that it becomes *part of the performance*. Curiously, though, while side-cameras frequently turn on the front-row audiences (and not only when they are being called into the action), the rest display

DOI: 10.1057/9781137288691

greater fixedness. There are long-held shots of the entire stage, captured from front-centre, with relatively few two-shots and semi-close-ups. Only one bravura filming moment stood out. When Corden's Franco debates increasingly desperately between his two employers' demands, the vision cut back and forth with increasingly speed, matching each of his bewildered turns and twists, ending with him punching himself in comical confusion. This intensification was special to the cinema audiences. This aside, camerawork was surprisingly undemonstrative. One moment encapsulated this. When an ancient butler tremulously carries a tray across the stage, cutlery vibrating, his slow passage was filmed in an entirely unaccentuated way. It was almost as though a decision had been taken on this occasion not to give any 'extras' to external audiences.

With livecast theatre, then, presentational structure appears to be a balancing act between wide stage-shots (to maintain a sense of overall production design, and to convey blocking), two-shots (for key dialogue scenes), and semi-close-ups (close enough to make monologues and moments of focused emotion emphatic, but 'semi' for the sake of theatre's larger bodily gestures). To these can be added judiciously chosen bravura moments created by editing, dissolves, and camera movements. These must vary by genre, of course. But a distinction is strictly maintained between front-of-stage and to-camera. Sound, by contrast, is much further from cinematic or even televisual manipulations and emphases.

Creating an opera aesthetic

With opera, of necessity, this presentational structure must be different. If peak emotion in theatre can be conveyed in near close-up on faces and bodily stances (within the enlargements required by stage conventions), in opera close-ups carry the risk of embarrassing epiglottalitis, as performers put their all into open-mouthed voice-maximisation. Here, too, of course genre is critical. Comic opera works more through characterisation, interactions, and stage movements, while tragic opera achieves its peaks in more static orchestra–voice combinations. Further, opera just is much more stylised. To the challenges of voice-projection into vast auditoria (remember the Met's house size) must be added the urge to spectacle (grand sets and lighting displays), exotic costuming and surging, often dance-inspired, movements in the set scenes. All classical opera also depends upon a set of stage conventions about seeing and hearing, nicely shown in a scene in *Anna Bolena* in which one character sings out a full-throated warning to another, 'Be silent! Someone may hear you!', on a stage full of actors. Opera carries the challenge that, while the music and voices are its cornerstone, acting and staging have to fit and extend them. What audiovisual capture may then do efficiently with these is the question.

A brief review of three New York Met livecasts, then: Mozart's comic opera *Don Pasquale*, Donizetti's gothic *Lucia di Lammermoor*, and the tragic *Anna Bolena* (based on the final days in the life of Anne Boleyn). All the Met's livecasts open with a mix of slides of forthcoming performances, invitations to join or support the Met, thanks to sponsors, and grandeur shots of the auditorium. Cinema audiences get taken backstage, both before (with rather gooey interviews with directors and singers) and between acts (to watch scene-changes, and to observe singers congratulating each other after complicated duets). Performances are subtitled (as indeed the house itself is surtitled), giving enough to allow story-following. Sound-capture is clearly critical to opera, and unobtrusive miking of performers allows them to be 'perfectly' balanced both with each other and against the orchestra (while the audience remains ambient background, even for comic opera).

Simplest was the broadly comedic *Don Pasquale*, with its story of a vain rich elderly man hoping to marry a beautiful young woman who, with her doctor-brother and lover-to-be Antonio, cozens him. The decorative set was brightly lit throughout the production. Using up to eight cameras (sides, front and high), camerawork mixed stage-shots and two-shots with occasional whole-body shots of individual singers. Dissolves were never used, and there were no bravura camera moments (it could reasonably be said that the most unusual camera-angles were reserved for observing scene-changes, with cameras high in the flies). The nearest to strong overt emotion was Antonio's long solo, as he sings his feelings of lost love. This was captured in a series of head and torso shots (always slightly canted), with sporadic reminders of the full stage. The distinction of front-of-stage and to-camera was strictly maintained throughout. Only rarely did editing separate and accentuate the artificiality of a singer's 'aside' to the audience (as when, for instance, the doctor sings of on-stage Pasquale 'Just you wait, you little miser – I'll show you a thing or two'). There were occasional moments when it seemed as if singers moved to sweet spots to allow nice side-angled two-shots (which would not be meaningful in the auditorium). Scenes with numbers of servants tended to combine

DOI: 10.1057/9781137288691

full-stage shots with occasional travelling shots, as if tracking along a chorus-line. In one, post-marriage scene there was a sense of the camera favouring a 'star': four singers in a line across stage-front are interweaving their parts, but the camera favoured the singer Anna Netrebko, although her part was no larger. With *Don Pasquale*, we might say in summary that camerawork aimed to be undemonstrative and unobtrusive.

The same is not true of *Lucia*. Here, sets were dark (as were costumes), and lighting created pools of visibility which cameras could accentuate – played upon by dressing the ghost in silvery-white. From the opening hunting scene, many shots from below isolated and accentuated lead singers. Here, too, scene-changes were strongly marked by travelling shots. Cameras caught and isolated moments of star-drama, as when Lucia – forced to marry by her brother – is thrown to the floor and weeps. These aside, this relatively immobile production was mirrored by a certain cinematic stiffness, with most expressive work done by lighting. Perhaps the nearest to a bravura shot came when the Pastor enters with the news that Lucia has killed her new husband in a frenzy. As he sings the events, a long-held shot wound in to a near close-up, then backed away again, cutting to a sliding shot down a stairway lined with listening guests (otherwise, this production did not really do reactions).

Anna Bolena, too, offered dark but sumptuous sets and costumes, lit to establish some strong contrasts of colour, but with less sense of camerawork then working to isolate characters within the overall stage. Much of the filming was in fact quite static, from stage-front. But following introductory interviews which forewarned audiences that the role of Anna was particularly challenging – and therefore there would be no interval interview with the singer (again, Netrebko) – as star of the show she was then permitted, in some of her solos, to sing virtually to camera, despite the fact that, perhaps partly because of the nature of the opera, acting as a means to express emotions is hardly visible (this is even stated by Anna, who declares: 'My grief is not on my face, it is deep in my heart').

In sum, then, we might reasonably characterise the Met's principles as *cautious*. There are bonuses, if you want them, for cinema audiences, in the form of slightly breathless (both literally, as they catch performers coming off stage, and figuratively, in their celebratory tones) interviews, in some participatory filming of the orchestra for the overtures and in the views of back-stage work. But the cinematic capture almost consciously avoids adding much except some 'star moments'.

DOI: 10.1057/9781137288691

Future studies

This account of the emergent aesthetics of livecasts is clearly limited by the number it considers, and also by their origins. All the plays are from the National Theatre, and all the operas from the New York Met. I have considered no other kinds: ballet, comedy, jazz or other kinds of music. And, of course, all my case-studies come from a period in which professional expertise is still being developed and tested. In the final chapter I pose a few questions which strike me as potentially of value. But I await with interest the examinations of other scholars, who will doubtless have questions of their own.

Notes

1   An interesting test case is the livecast of Arnold Wesker's *The Kitchen*. Watching this, I was struck by a powerful opening shot. The camera travelled around the circular stage-set, moving between ovens and food preparation points, showing details to cinema audiences. Having toured, it then retreated to a front-of-stage position *before* the first actor entered. One suspects that this was tolerable to the theatre audience because the move was completed before the play began – except, of course, that for cinema audiences in important senses the play thus *began several minutes earlier*.

2   One such drop-out certainly occurred in *Phèdre* when a maid crossed a dead area.

3   The one exception to this, a half-glance at camera by the Creature, actually looked unintended.

4   A still from this arrival provides a striking frontispiece to NT Live's (2010) evaluation of its first two livecast seasons.

DOI: 10.1057/9781137288691

3
A Portrait of Livecasts' Audiences

Abstract: *Summarising the evidence on who the audiences for livecasts are and in what ways they enjoy them, this chapter draws on research by the National Endowment for Science, Technology and the Arts, Picturehouse Cinemas, the New York Met and the author's own survey. Clear and unexpected patterns emerge, including that of older audiences returning to the cinema for these events, and engaging committedly and emotionally with them. The chapter shows and explores two broad kinds of response, 'Expert' and 'Immersive' orientations, which have quite opposite and indeed conflicting expectations of these events.*

Barker, Martin. *Live To Your Local Cinema: The Remarkable Rise of Livecasting*. Basingstoke: Palgrave Macmillan, 2013. DOI: 10.1057/9781137288691.

Who goes to these livecasts, then? What do they want, expect and get out of them? And in what ways is watching them at a cinema like and unlike watching them at source? We can paint quite a detailed portrait of the audiences for livecasts by drawing on the overlapping findings of four bodies of research: from the UK's National Endowment for Science, Technology and the Arts (NESTA), the New York Met, Picturehouse Cinemas and my own. NESTA compared responses between 1,316 cinemagoers with 1,216 theatregoers watching *Phèdre*. In the largest research exercise to date, the New York Met gathered 5,306 responses to a survey distributed to cinemas which were screening HD transmissions of their operas. Picturehouse conducted research among those on their email list, for the performances of *Ondine* (178 responses) and, more generally, for the Met Opera season (856 responses). (Picturehouse also gave me access to the raw data from their research, which allowed me to search it in my own ways, and make some additional discoveries.) My own research recruited 644 respondents to an online questionnaire with linked quantitative and qualitative questions. In broad terms, the five bodies of research appear broadly to confirm each other. Each, however, asks some questions that the others do not.

Pause to think about the sheer quantity of this early research. Consider NESTA. Founded in 1998, and funded by Lottery money, NESTA presented itself as the UK's leading non-governmental promoter of innovation, and supporter of new technological advances and 'creative pioneers'.[1] Very much a creature of New Labour thinking, NESTA put a heavy focus on the idea of the 'creative industries', and also worked on areas of 'social exclusion' (on the politics of this, see Garnham, 2005). Its work threaded together policy-makers, government departments, academic researchers and business entrepreneurs. It not only supported particular business ventures which approached it with viable ideas, but also promoted research, on the back of which (to quote its 2004 Annual Report) 'having identified important gaps in the system, we shared our insights with other funders and policymakers at a seminar in April this year, following which we are developing policy proposals in conversation with key players across the UK' (NESTA, 2004).

In July 2008 NESTA launched 'Take 12 – Digital Innovation in Film', a project run in association with the UK Film Council and 12 small companies to 'explore how small creative businesses can exploit the opportunities provided by digital technology' (NESTA, 2004). This was part of a rising tide of enthusiasm for the emerging potentials of digitising

DOI: 10.1057/9781137288691

cinemas – one which could quickly lose its gloss, as 3D would show (Stewart, 2010). NESTA was keen to build a business model for livecasts, to measure that potential (Bakhshi and Throsby, 2009). It therefore commissioned research into audiences for NT Live's first livecast, *Phèdre*.

Conducted at considerable cost (it involved employing people to capture questionnaire responses at a number of cinemas showing NT Live events), the research was made available to sponsors in a provisional form, and then released more widely as 'Beyond Live' (NESTA, 2010). NESTA asked people 31 multiple-choice questions, including how they had heard about the event; their reasons for where they chose to watch it (distance, cost, etc.); whether they had sought out information about the play and performance in advance; their main interest in it (its liveness, Helen Mirren's presence, the play, the general ambience, or because another person had persuaded them to go); their hopes and expectations for the performance – and their feelings when they saw it (measured along 13 dimensions); the price ranges for theatre and cinema; whether they expected to attend more such events; and some personal information (sex, income, educational level, and whether they had any working connections with theatre or cinema).

'Beyond Live' headlines its most important findings. Cinema attracted attenders from a wider economic spectrum than the theatre. Their sources of information were notably different: cinemagoers depended much more on local (cinema) publicity. While 60 per cent of theatre visitors nominated Mirren as their prime motive for going, the single most common cinemagoers' choice (at 38 per cent) was attraction to a new way of seeing theatre. 'Intriguingly, despite lower expectations, cinema audiences reported higher levels of emotional engagement with the production than those who experienced the play at the National Theatre.' For both audiences, a sense of its 'liveness' was an overwhelmingly (above 80 per cent) important part of their enjoyment (and there was little interest in buying DVDs of productions).

To the authors of the Report, the most distinctive finding was that 'digital innovation was enabling the National Theatre to reach new audiences'. This in a way is both the whole point – and also the limitation – of the research, that it can 'aid the competitive success of the UK's creative industries'. From a different perspective, of wanting to understand these experiences *per se*, there were wasted opportunities here. For instance, while the authors report their important finding that cinemas are recruiting economically more diverse audiences, they do not go on to explore

DOI: 10.1057/9781137288691

any ways in which this widened audience might differ in its responses. Do the new audiences draw on the same sources of knowledge, are their expectations the same, and what kinds of appreciation and involvement do they display? Or again, while the authors report that cinema audiences draw on word-of-mouth considerably more than theatre audiences, they do not, for instance, ask how this relates to another finding, that cinema audiences are more likely to want to discuss their experiences afterwards. It is indeed striking that cinema audiences give higher ratings than theatre audiences on measures of absorption, emotional response and intellectual engagement – but then surely it would be worth knowing more about this group. For instance, is such raised involvement concentrated in those lower income groups? Because of its business orientation, there is unsurprisingly a considerable interest in what people are willing to pay for the theatrical and cinema experiences. Although the point is not commented on in the Report, it appears these audiences do not use ordinary cinema prices as their measure of expectations for these events. So again it would have been interesting to know whether there was any discrepancy in attitudes to pricing between those who reported that they would or would not attend such events at their local cinema. These are among the many missed opportunities resulting from not exploring the data in any depth, and instead just garnering beneficial boosterist headlines.[2]

Let us put NESTA, and its research, in a larger context. There has been a general rise in research designed to evaluate the economic and cultural benefits of the arts. Elsewhere in the UK, the now-defunct UK Film Council funded research into both the cultural (see Narval Media et al., 2009; Northern Alliance and Ipsos MediaCT, 2011) and the economic benefits of the film industry (see Oxford Economics, 2007). These reports ranged widely across kinds of potential value, from the ways a sample of films present 'the British' to themselves and others, to their box office achievements and wider cultural resonances. They did not, sadly, explore the ways in which different kinds of audience have responded to these films. Another report direct to Government at least considered how such research might be done, even if it did not do any (O'Brien, 2010). But the UK was not alone in this surge of interest in 'valuing the arts'. In the different context of America, another project tried to do this for the arts generally. Commissioned by a consortium of 14 university arts presenters, Alan Brown and Jennifer Novak (2007) from the WolfBrown Research Institute evaluated the methods and benefits of studying 'the intrinsic impacts of a live performance'.[3] Their Report makes clear that

DOI: 10.1057/9781137288691

their main motive was to provide evidence of the value of the arts that goes beyond the anecdotal ('This novel/play/poem changed my life') and transcends the commercial ('Theatre generates this amount of money'). The research was conducted among operatic, dance, theatrical and musical audiences. It is interesting that the indices Brown and Novak used (very similar to NESTA's: captivation, intellectual stimulation, emotional resonance, spiritual value, aesthetic growth and social bonding) all sound like unarguably good things – although it would not take much pushing to see that the same qualities might not be so valued in popular culture (with 'captivation' becoming 'mindless absorption', 'resonance' becoming the more troubling 'identification', and 'social bonding' raising issues of *whom* we are bonding with). From this and other researches, it is clear that the value of the arts and the potential of new media within these were becoming hot topics. (For useful overviews of these developments in the UK, see Keaney, 2008; Rumbold, 2008; O'Reilly and Kerrigan, 2012.)[4] I return to the broader ramifications of this in Chapter 6.

A first portrait of livecast audiences

The first striking thing is to note is the age spread of those attending. Figure 3.1 displays the age distribution among my 644 respondents.

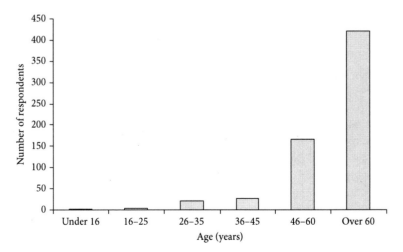

FIGURE 3.1 *Age of audience*
Source: author's data.

DOI: 10.1057/9781137288691

Evidence embedded within the New York Met's responses largely confirms this, with just slightly higher proportions of younger audiences. (There are indications from other countries that these patterns may not be universal. Anecdotally, I hear from Australia that livecasts there may attract a younger audience. This prompts me to acknowledge that a great deal of my evidence comes from the UK, and to await with real interest research from other countries.) Striking in itself, this age profile becomes all the more significant when compared with the almost exactly opposite age profile of cinema audiences generally. Livecasts seem to be attracting audiences back to the cinema who may otherwise attend rarely or not at all. But of course older audiences are differently invested in culture. They are likely to make different kinds of demands (facilities, information, environment) of the venues they attend. Financial decisions are more planned. The implications of these differences are rarely explored. Indeed, for reasons bound up perhaps with who researchers are, and what our research priorities have been, mature audiences have hardly come up for consideration.

An indicator of one difference associated with this particular older audience emerges from my re-analysis of Picturehouse's New York Met data. Within their 856 respondents, 662 declared very high or high levels of engagement with the event. When we look within this engaged group, two further things become evident. First, this committed group was *older* than the already age-skewed overall set. A re-analysis of the data reveals that the older the audience, the more likely they are to declare high levels of engagement (with the over-60s constituting just 47 per cent of their respondents, but 69 per cent of the most engaged). Second, this group is markedly more interested in attending other – even pre-recorded – events. My hunch is that this marks this group's interest in having a wide range of cultural activities to hand now that they are in retirement.

The gender balance also reverses cinema attendance patterns, with (in my sample) 70.7 per cent women to 39.3 per cent men. NESTA matched these figures for cinema attendance closely (72.3 per cent women to 27.7 per cent men) but, curiously, found a much more balanced attendance at the theatre (50.9 per cent women to 49.1 per cent men). The cinema difference gains importance when cross-tabulated with interest in attending other events: for all four kinds of event about which I asked, women were more likely than men to want to attend as often as possible (see Table 3.1).

NESTA compared income levels of those attending the National Theatre with income levels of those attending cinema screenings: '24.5

per cent of cinemagoers earned less than £20,000 per year, compared with only 15.8 per cent of those who attended *Phèdre* at the National Theatre. The share of cinemagoers with incomes above £50,000 per year, at 12.9 per cent, was half as much as at the theatre.' NESTA's figures do also, if unsurprisingly, suggest there remains a strong overall middle-class bias among both cinema and theatre audiences.[5]

People went to the cinema for somewhat different reasons than to the theatre. As we've seen, NESTA found that, while over 60 per cent of their *Phèdre* theatre audience gave seeing Helen Mirren as their prime reason (a curious inversion, one might say, of presumed balances of interest in celebrities), the cinema audience gave a much wider spread of answers, with the highest percentage saying that it was the chance to try out a theatrical experience in a new environment. Surprisingly, NESTA did not consider the possible implication that this was a novelty impulse which might not lead to a regular interest. My differently constructed dataset did partly answer this. In Table 3.2, a cross-tabulation of responses to

TABLE 3.1 *Relationship between sex and frequency of attending (%)*

Attend as often as possible	Male	Female
Ballet	4.8	9.2
Cinema	14.3	18.9
Opera	36.5	42.2
Theatre	14.7	22.5

Source: author's data.

TABLE 3.2 *Relationship between number of experiences and judgement of event*

	First experience	Once previously	Twice previously	More than twice previously
Excellent	61.9%	51.9%	65.4%	66.2%
Good	28.6%	42.3%	21.2%	29.3%
Average	5.4%	5.8%	7.7%	3.4%
Poor	5.4%	0.0%	5.8%	0.6%
Very poor	0.0%	0.0%	0.0%	0.4%
Total number of responses	56	52	52	474

Source: author's data.

DOI: 10.1057/9781137288691

two questions (levels of approval of the attended performance and prior experience of attending such events) shows a curious pattern.

The sizeable drop in ratings between first and second experiences, coupled with evidence from discursive responses, leads me to think that a number of people tried the experience once and gave it the benefit of the doubt,[6] tried it once more less enthusiastically (now having a point of comparison), and then may select themselves out. The ones who return have fallen in love with this mode of encountering theatre and opera *because of* its differences – thence the rise in ratings with the greater the number of experiences. The question will shortly be: what are those differences perceived to be?

The novelty factor may be important in other, more complicated ways. Evidence from the New York Met's research, among others, indicates that these events attract some audiences who may not otherwise attend such performances: 'Nearly one in five (18%)…have not been to a live opera in the last two years. This suggests that the transmissions do bring a significant number of people not currently attending live performances to performances. Nevertheless, the core audience remains moderate opera goers (35% attended live opera 1–4 times in the last two years) and frequent opera goers (47% attended live opera 5 or more times in the last two years, with 25% attending 10 or more).' The sensitivity evidenced here towards more established audiences of course has implications for the ways of managing and presenting these events. Producers must be careful not to offend more traditionalist attendees by too much stylistic innovation.

Audience pleasures and meanings

As Figure 3.2 shows, livecasts were highly rated.

These numbers hide some significant complexities, including some emergent disappointments. But before we come to those, add in that striking feature from NESTA's research. NESTA asked its audiences how high their expectations had been in advance, and then gauged levels of involvement on a series of measures (e.g. absorption, emotional and cognitive engagement, being transported, creative stimulation, sensing others responding and excitement at the event's liveness[7]). On all measures cinema audiences gave more positive responses, sometimes almost double those of the theatre audience – including most strikingly to the 'liveness' question. We will see in the next chapter what might lie behind this.

DOI: 10.1057/9781137288691

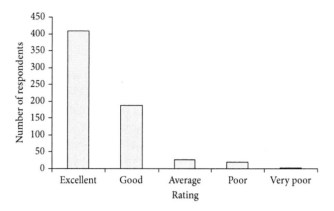

FIGURE 3.2   *Overall ratings of quality of event*
Source: author's data.

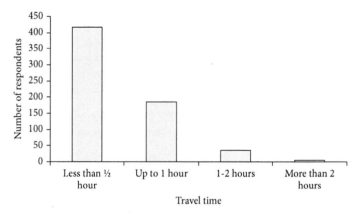

FIGURE 3.3   *Approximate time to reach event*
Source: author's data.

In a number of ways, audience responses display a strong sense of the value of *localness*. The first and most obvious way is in the clear finding in my results that people did not by and large travel very far to reach the cinema screening (see Figure 3.3).

Curiously, a closer examination of my data revealed that the place in the UK where people travelled furthest to attend a livecast was London – hinting at the possibility that, here at least, audiences either had failed to obtain tickets to the source-event or were generally willing to travel greater distances for their cultural experiences (and available transport

DOI: 10.1057/9781137288691

services may assist this). But alongside these quantitative measures, qualitative responses show that for many people particular cinemas can add further, special senses of *localness*:

> It was a fantastic performance in excellent quality at a local cinema in great comfort with friends. [302][8]

> It's comfortable in the cinema and you get a great view of the auditorium too at the beginning. Our local cinema has a good system for ordering drinks for the interval which is great. The only thing you miss out on is the excitement of a live event but actually it was pretty exciting at our cinema – everyone clapped at the end! [106]

> We are opera fans and spending half our time far away it is great to be able to access it in a local cinema. [72]

Sometimes this sense of belonging could erupt into revealing complaints about the wrong kinds of audience spoiling people's enjoyment:

> Unfortunately at [my cinema] the audience seems probably to be mostly composed of 3rd rate Academics, local Government bods and others who have had a cushioned life-style. They are all so uptight and refuse to clap at the big moments and join in the experience. I think Academics in particular should be charged double and then they might appreciate what is on offer. [386]

What this begins to reveal is that some people may wish to *own* a local space. And, beyond this, a local cinema might become a different kind of cultural site:

> Nothing could improve the experience in a good quality cinema like the Picturehouse at all. All the better points were that the Picturehouse is comfortable (luxurious seating), clean and the staff are welcoming; there isn't the snobbery that there is at the Opera House and you can still feel part of the production by dressing up just as you would at the Theatre. [526]

'Ownership' for some people clearly extends to a sense that the cinema is more culturally welcoming to 'their kind' than theatres or opera houses. What this leads to, at its best, is a powerful sense of participating in the *occasion*. People feel it is theirs, in all senses. This is caught in these ordinary but important responses:

> I had a bottle of wine and my wife beside me and a good view of the action ... with superb sound to boot. [33]

> I liked the whole experience feeling you're part of such a huge global event. My mother was watching in Montreal while I was in Oxford. [554]

DOI: 10.1057/9781137288691

For a few, this sense of a special experience then spilled out to make the local a place for being anything but local, as here:

> Wonderful life-enhancing experience. In these very doom-laden times (dire political situation nationally and internationally etc) and with toxic/mediocre television programming (reality shows, Jeremy Kyle etc), it was magical to be enjoying beautiful music in such an immediate close-up way, and to know that others in 40 countries were also enjoying it at the same time. [166]

In my final chapter I explore the implications in this kind of response for thinking about 'high culture' experiences, so clearly differentiated from the 'toxic' and the 'mediocre'.

Differentiating the audience

Livecasts have to date been concentrated mainly in three art-forms: opera, theatre and (to a lesser extent) ballet. It is interesting to ask how audiences for these three relate to each other, in light of the extensive debates that have followed the work of French cultural sociologist Pierre Bourdieu on the culture-class affiliations of different art-forms, and associated ways of participating. Bourdieu (1979) argued, influentially, that cultural tastes are broadly aligned with class memberships, and that there are, for each distinct level of taste, 'relatively stable dispositions' through which people's reactions to any particular art-form or cultural practice will be shaped. This is the heart of his concept of 'habitus' – a concept which itself embraces both how we learn about culture and how our bodies have learnt to respond. Bourdieu offers a broad distinction between a knowing and distanced way of *looking at* culture, which he regarded as characteristic of 'high culture', and an enthusiast and participative mode, which characterises low or popular culture. Bourdieu's claims have been widely debated, but here I am concerned only with that claim of the *relative stability* of responses which underscores his picture of 'habitus'. One critic in particular, Bernard Lahire (2003), has challenged Bourdieu's account on this point, arguing for a far more individualised account – yet still, curiously, tending to assume that *within individuals* responses to all forms of culture will tend to be unified. The same problem inheres in another set of debates about Bourdieu's work, this time focused on his claim that those in the highest culture-class segregate themselves within those forms and contexts which most allow those distanced forms of appreciation. For instance, two American

DOI: 10.1057/9781137288691

sociologists of music, Peterson and Kern (1996), drew on American survey evidence to argue that high-culture 'univores' have been replaced by 'omnivores': the wealthy and powerful now being willing to enjoy *all* forms of culture, including rock music, jazz and pop (although Biron, 2009, has pointed out how loose their categories are – for instance, their treatment of 'jazz' as a unitary entity).

Although, as will be clear in my penultimate chapter, I find Bourdieu's general approach to the idea of cultural taste systems valuable, I want here to question these claims, on two grounds. First, my evidence indicates quite sharp taste differentiations among the audiences for the three core streamed forms. While theatre and opera show reasonably strong overlaps, ballet seems to occupy a specialist area, with its own, rather distinct audience. I asked people to say how frequently they would try to attend ballet, cinema, opera and theatre. Mapping these responses against each other revealed that while the combination of cinema, theatre and opera produced 193 saying that they would attend 'As Often As Possible' or 'Frequently', all the combinations which included ballet produced falls of around 75 per cent. This suggests that ballet belongs in a rather separate and specialist domain for most people.

But, further to this, it became clear that people attended even the two more popular events, theatre and opera, with different expectations and criteria. Strikingly, opera-lovers love performances *per se*. Even limiting myself to unambiguous answers, I found that 171 (30.4 per cent) of those responding to the opera performances opened their answers by declaring an overall commitment to the medium ('I/we love opera', 'I'm an opera fan/nut', 'We are passionate about opera'). This figure would have been much higher if I had counted even slightly more complicated answers (for instance, those declaring a love of Verdi or Strauss, or of classical music as a whole).

No such pattern is to be found for theatre. Just eight responses (10 per cent of the total) opened with such a declaration. Instead, people were much more likely to single out the *company* ('We love NT productions') or *Shakespeare*, or to make a point of saying they liked *good quality theatre* ('Heard it was a good production'). With theatre, the emphasis appears to be more on a guarantee that the production will be of trusted quality and value. A historically sharper line between professional and amateur theatre, and the associated dreads of Am-Dram, school plays, good or bad pantomimes and the like, along with perhaps an insistent differentiation of serious theatre from West End popular shows, have,

DOI: 10.1057/9781137288691

it seems, sedimented into a wish for foreknowledge of the quality of a theatre production. Hence, interestingly, there are more references in people's answers on theatre to *reviews*, as in these:

> Enjoy Shakespeare. Play had good reviews. Easy to get to. [14]

> I'd read the reviews and it was supposed to be a good production of the play which is not often performed. [154]

> Enjoyment of theatre and especially Shakespeare. Reviews of London production very good. Not had chance to go to the National to see it. [619]

Answers such as these strongly suggest a difference in the way people commit to the two forms. Opera is loved as a whole by many, who may then indicate preferences. It's not difficult to think of some contributory reasons. Opera has a much less developed amateur tradition than theatre. There are simply fewer venues and performances, professional or otherwise. But my sense is that this is not the whole. Opera performances *per se* are a passion for a substantial number of these people. Theatre on the other hand is sought out when it is expected to be good. The significance of this can be confirmed by asking whether the group declaring 'I'm an opera fan' (or something similar) were distinct in other ways from the overall contingent of opera visitors. They were, in small but striking ways. People describing themselves in this manner were more likely to rate a performance Excellent (67.1 per cent v. 55.8 per cent) and more likely to have attended more than two livecasts (88.8 per cent v. 77.3 per cent) than others.

These results suggest that audiences may engage with theatre and opera in pretty distinct ways. This has challenging implications not just for Peterson and Kern, but for other undifferentiating accounts of cultural participation.

An overview of Alternative Content audiences

With caution, what can we say overall about the emergent' audiences for livecasts? They are overwhelmingly not traditional cinema audiences. Older, and with different cultural interests, they are demanding, and likely to become increasingly so. They like the 'local' aspect of seeing livecasts at the cinema. Of course differentiated (it is pretty much the first rule of audience research that it finds differences, disqualifying lazy talk of 'the audience'), nonetheless, there are signs of sedimenting enthusiasm, a learning of new manners of participation and – surely to

DOI: 10.1057/9781137288691

come – an emergent set of aesthetic judgements and criteria. Early over-all willingness to try events is likely to move towards greater selectivity.

This is a highly unusual audience, from a research point of view. It is not simply that, as a number of critics have pointed out, for a long time cultural studies had a fascination with youth, on some unstated assumption that they were more important because, perhaps, more radical. Academic studies of older audiences are few and far between. Marketing studies of them tend to be interested only in the relationship between their purchasing choices and their class-cultural location (and poorer older people are pretty much invisible).[9] But it is more than the simple demographic. This audience reveals itself to be a very particular *kind* of audience. They are mature, self-aware, knowledgeable, alert to the nature of these occasions, aware of each other and much taken by this develop-ment. They are also literate, self-confident, assertive and sure in their judgements and place in the world.

As a particularly aware audience, one prominent feature of their response to livecasts is the combination of rich appreciation of the chance to see fine performances (for instance, note the combination of positiv-ity and politeness in this: 'This was our first visit to live Met Opera and we felt privileged to have such an impressive facility in Henley. We shall certainly go again. Thank you') with a matching assertion of what the viewing environment should be like. Here is an assemblage of comments drawn from Picturehouse's New York Met responses, all (including the one above) culled from people who gave high ratings to the event, and all from responses to my final question asking whether respondents had any other comments:

> I welcome this opportunity to make comments in the hope that you will be encouraged to continue. Fortunately I am very fortunate to have a very patient carer to accompany me to the performance but the limited space of the foyer and the refreshment bar makes it rather chaotic. Uniformed stewards may help. ... Temperature up in cinema, it was really cold. Bell/reminder of some sort towards end of intervals. ... Before the opera screening screen a brief summary of the opera with pictures of the main characters and their (opera) names. For me this would help knowing who was which foreigner. ... Somewhere to leave coats would be good. ... Quick + easy drink/food at intervals would be welcome when it's so busy and with short breaks only available. Appreciate the synopsis you provide. ... Stop latecomers entering. Stop disrupting folk leaving while opera is being shown. ... Ban pop corn! ... Having designated seats is impor-tant! ... Encourage clapping? And dressing up??? A pity your foyer is so small

DOI: 10.1057/9781137288691

and crowded. ... No awful canned music in the foyer area would be really appreciated. Silence is golden! ... Dedicated space and staff for interval refreshments needed at Greenwich Picturehouse. At the Macbeth performance there was not even milk available for coffee!! ... I think a club could be formed for enthusiasts to discuss the performance after the show or a meeting before the showing and a speaker or lecture in the bar. ... Sell wine that is pleasant to drink. The Shiraz we had last time was terrible.

These are people who think they have something to add to the experience, and think it right and proper to say this.

This audience is very particular. It knows what it likes, and it knows the conditions under which it expects to get it. It likes quality and has a strong sense (even with all the disagreements over particulars) of what this amounts to. This has sizeable implications for the providing cinemas (present and future), apart from anything else.

Notes

1   This relationship with government was subtly revealed in October 2010 when the NESTA website carried a report welcoming the decision by the new Government to grant NESTA 'full independence', moving it from public to charitable status.

2   I had hoped that I would be able to access NESTA's raw data to try to answer these questions for myself. Unfortunately in the end these were never made available to me.

3   Interestingly, this research is cited by O'Brien as a model of how to do such audience research (see also Radbourne et al., 2010). Also, in early 2011, a major initiative was launched in the UK by the New Economics Foundation to encourage theatres to increase the extent and depth of their audience research, in order to demonstrate the many benefits that theatre can bring to audiences (see New Economics Foundation, 2011).

4   For other research evidently driven by this search for a new warranty for investment in the arts, see the Arts Council Report 'Arts Audiences: Insight' (2008), which proffers a model of the different kinds of audiences the arts might attract, based on Experian/MOSAIC-style postcode consumer research. Another, slightly more indirect, but still relevant, example is the evaluation research conducted on the impact of the TV series *Operatunity* by Marion Friend (2003), from Diverse Ltd. Funded by the Arts Council under its Gateway 5 programme (for encouraging new audiences and thereby proving the arts' value to Britain), the research documented the stages,

DOI: 10.1057/9781137288691

participants and, most emphatically, the press coverage and other debates which the series elicited. The final paragraph captures its overall promotional tone: 'The result is an absolutely fascinating, funny, and emotive series, thanks in no small part to the applicants themselves. The human story is riveting. It's clear from the start that the applicants are mostly passionate about opera, and many of them have wanted to become singers their whole lives but, for a variety of reasons, were never given a chance. It meant that having to tell people they hadn't made it through to the next stage got increasingly hard. Yet their generosity of spirit was extraordinary, and they were pleased for those who had been successful even when they were very upset.'

5   It was difficult to extrapolate a clear picture, because NESTA used very wide income bands (under £10,000, £10,000–20,000, £20,000–50,000, over £50,000 per annum). Also, more than 25 per cent declined to answer their question on this.

6   Many of my respondents were acutely aware of this being their first time, and credited it with extra just for that, as here: 'This was our first experience of such a performance, we have nothing else to compare it with but loved every moment' [298]. It is the awareness of a lack of points of comparison which is striking here.

7   Pretty evidently, this set of ways of measuring aspects of responses owes much to the ideas of Brown and Novak (2007).

8   Bracketed numbers after each quotation indicate the respondent's position within the research database.

9   For a clear example of this kind of interest, see Rick Poynor's (2001) *Obey the Giant*, which explores in considerable detail the marketing research which underpinned the development of Britain's largest-ever shopping complex, Bluewater: 'Early research by Lend Lease, the Australian owners of Bluewater, showed that nine million people live within an hour's drive of the site, and they are among Britain's wealthiest consumers, with an annual expenditure 32% higher than the national average. Four out of five fall into the A, B, or C socio-economic groups used by marketers. Over 72% of those homes are owner-occupied and have access to a car. Further research, in the form of a questionnaire, led to the division of this catchment into seven clusters, accounting for almost five million people. These categories were given names to reflect their lifestyle characteristics. Highest in spending power, and therefore of greatest interest to Bluewater's developers, were the "County Classics" (wealthy, usually married, wide interests, concerned with home, entertaining, family and quality); the "Club Executives" (successful, married, quality-conscious, like to be in control, prepared to pay extra for convenience); and the "Young Fashionables" (single, early twenties, image-conscious, brand-oriented, active). All three groups preferred to do "serious" shopping in central London.' (2001:26)

DOI: 10.1057/9781137288691

4

The Many Meanings of 'Liveness'

Abstract: *The notion of 'liveness' has been endowed with importance in a wide range of intellectual fields, including most importantly theatre and performance studies, film studies, television studies, comedy studies, virtual performance studies and sports studies (with smaller debates within music, and most specifically opera, studies). But each of these fields has debated this topic in almost entire ignorance of other fields' debates. Through a comparison of the debates, this chapter shows 'liveness' to be multi-dimensional, with each of the fields valuing different dimensions.*

Barker, Martin. *Live To Your Local Cinema: The Remarkable Rise of Livecasting*. Basingstoke: Palgrave Macmillan, 2013. DOI: 10.1057/9781137288691.

DOI: 10.1057/9781137288691

> I'm not saying that liveness is dying, but that it desperately needs a
> re-examination. We need a theatre in which liveness is interrogated,
> integrated and integral; a theatre that truly values its own liveness and
> couldn't exist without it. A Liveness 2.0, if you will.
>
> (Trueman, 2009)

This comment from a theatre reviewer nicely evokes the tensions inside
a debate which has ruffled the surface of theatre criticism for some years
now. Strongly normative ('we need…truly values'), horribly aware of
unstoppable changes ('Liveness 2.0'), Trueman is on the hunt for some
distinguishing characteristic which will be theatre's grounds of defence
and validation. The prompt for his article was the challenge of livecasts.
And they do lay down a challenge. Certainly the experience is simul-
taneous with the event. But there is no physical co-presence. Audience
responses cannot be heard by performers. There can be no interaction. In
between audience and performance comes a whole apparatus of capture,
with technical, professional and aesthetic choices pre-formed for audiences. Yet in many ways, audiences at livecasts do value their as-liveness.

In 2009 Picturehouse asked their subscribers directly about this.[1] They
asked people to indicate their levels of interest in attending a whole range
of possible kinds of Alternative Content presentation – some of which
had not yet been tried (for instance, cookery master-classes). They then
asked them to say as well how interested they would be in attending if
the presentation was not live, but transmitted 24 hours later. In every
case, for every kind of presentation, levels of interest fell by almost 50
per cent for the delayed transmissions. Clearly, even if no other aspect
of liveness mattered to people, simultaneity does. And the industry has
learnt this. Dodona Research published a survey of the state of knowledge on Alternative Content in 2011 (Keeping and Grummit, 2011). It
contained a striking opposition. Across the period 2007–10, the propor-
tion of live transmissions had doubled from 26.0 per cent to 54.9 per
cent, while recorded transmissions had declined from 72 per cent to 42
per cent (the residue being mixed presentations). This was evidently an
industry learning fast, alert to emerging audience preferences. Yet in the
other direction, NT Live's (2010) self-evaluation noted: 'In the second
season, NT Live added some repeat screenings when demand exceeded
the capacity for the live screenings. Anecdotal feedback in non-live terri-
tories and for such repeat screenings has shown that the knowledge that
it was originally broadcast live seems to be a factor in its appeal, more

DOI: 10.1057/9781137288691

than if it had been distributed solely as a pre-recorded or edited version.' Clearly, 'liveness' – whatever it might mean – is pretty complex.

But what Trueman reveals, and what many other examples confirm, is the heavy valency which attaches to the idea of 'liveness'. This goes beyond simple likes and dislikes. Liveness matters. But *how* it matters varies mightily, I discovered, according to which area of public and academic thinking you turn to. An examination of those areas where significant debates can be discerned also shows that they are pretty much unaware of each other. At least seven almost hermetically sealed domains of thinking about liveness exist, then, in theatre and performance studies, television studies, film studies, comedy studies, music studies, virtual presence studies and sports studies. To these can be added occasional but important forays such as Andrew Crisell's (2012) impassioned plea for a return to 'liveness' in radio, and odd crossover subfields, such as one devoted to the study of karaoke performance (which straddles theatre and music, but appears to have its own vocabulary; see Brown, 2010, as an instance). In this chapter I visit each of the seven main domains to ask how 'liveness' is conceptualised, and what kind of an issue it is for each.

'Liveness' in theatre and performance studies

To understand the debate within theatre and performance, one has to recognise that in this domain academics run very close to professionals – especially where the more experimental forms of theatre and performance are concerned. Many academics not only teach and research; they also act, write and direct. When writing about theatre and performance, then, they do it with at least half an eye to practitioners' sense of their world.

Debates about 'liveness' date back at least to the 1950s, and to the rise of 'physical theatre', with its commitment to stripping performances of intrusive sets, costumes and the like, so that there was unfettered interaction between performers and their audiences. Debates around this became heightened in the 1980s as broader continental theories (for instance, deriving from Foucault) led to charges of over-simplification of ideas of 'presence'. This led eventually to a famous showdown between Peggy Phelan and Philip Auslander. Phelan, whose book *Unmarked* (1993) is a polemical feminist challenge, goes beyond simple norma- tive declarations to effectively preach a gospel of utopian performance, at whose epicentre is an idealised situation in which utterly engaged

DOI: 10.1057/9781137288691

viewer-participants are ready to have their identities altered. She writes, as though pronouncing a sermon:

> Performance's only life is in the present. Performance cannot be saved, recorded, documented, or otherwise participate in the circulation of representations *of* representations: once it does so, it becomes something other than performance. To the degree that performance attempts to enter the economy of reproduction it betrays and lessens the promise of its own ontology. (1993: 146)

This declarative manifesto was challenged by Phelan's colleague Philip Auslander's broad and influential book *Liveness* (1999). Auslander mounted a wide-ranging critique of those who 'reassert the integrity of the live' versus the 'corrupt, co-opted nature of the mediatized' (1999: 39). I have discussed Auslander's views in some detail before (Barker, 2003). Without rehearsing that entire argument, I repeat here a couple of key points. His general position is that the 'live' is historically and semiotically dependent on its opposite, the 'recorded': 'the live can only exist in a context where there is recording. It is a category of the not-recorded' (1999: 51). But there are tensions in Auslander's argument, tensions centred on some unstated assumptions about what it means to be 'mediated' or 'mediatized'.

Auslander's examples prove particularly telling. He recounts young people at a live rock concert being able to watch large-screen, close-up projections of what is happening on stage, and even being able to listen on headphones hooked directly into the bands' amplification systems. To Auslander, this clearly constitutes a *failure* of genuine liveness. This sees liveness as lack of technological intervention, rather than as, for instance, a mode of participation, even a sense of shared purpose. His account denies the possibility of *heightening* participation through technological means. The key lies in certain elements of Auslander's language which owe much to Roland Barthes and to Jean Baudrillard: in particular the idea of 'naturalising'. So, in another example, he cites Madonna wearing a virtually invisible head mike – calling this a 'naturalising' of her media-tised performance. The presumption is that this is an act of concealment whose function is to aid a *pretence* that the performance is not artificial. But if we were to redescribe the invisible head mike as permitting a 'less interrupted' or 'more uninhibited' performance, permitting her face to participate fully in the performance, the implications would change completely. We could then see Madonna as choosing technologies which can *complement*, rather than impede, her performance (Barker, 2003: 30)

DOI: 10.1057/9781137288691

There is, in fact, a deep pessimism in Auslander's argument. Those who do not fear the loss of liveness are at best missing out, at worst deceived, embroiled. At the end of his exposition, he poses a rhetorical question: 'I wonder whether having seen the live stage performance of *Beauty and the Beast*, for instance, counts more among children today than owning a copy of the movie on video cassette. What value will be attached to live performance when these generations attain cultural power?' (1999: 60). This is merchant-of-doom talk. It seems that, even in the most critically astute work in theatre and performance studies, there is a heavy investment in the need to defend 'liveness'. It is a primary cultural value, a *sine qua non*, of proper artistic experience.

There have been substantial debates around Auslander's work since its publication – many of them focused within the specific domain of performance theory and practice.[2] But one contribution particularly relevant to this book has come from Christopher Balme, who argues against what he sees as 'media essentialism' within these debates, whose longer history he delineates. Balme (2008b) argues instead for the idea of 'intermediality' – that is, that we live in a world of increasingly interpenetrative media which constantly cross-refer. Balme illustrates this argument with the early tale of Marcel Proust, who, in his final years, ensconced himself within a cork-lined room to exclude all noise – but kept up-to-date with contemporary Parisian theatre via a 'Theatrophone', a device which broadcast the sounds of performances. Balme is making the point that the crossing of media is hardly a new phenomenon. His focus in the end is on three particular performances to which interplay of media is key. But it is his general critique and its general implications which are most relevant here, as when he writes: 'The theatre spectator is a spectator with competence and knowledge in a variety of media. ... From the point of view of research, it is necessary to examine more closely different media aesthetics as a question of conventionality, i.e., as historically emergent practices of seeing, hearing and behaving rather than as essentialized properties determined by material factors' (2008b: 90). I return later to this concept of 'intermediality'.

For now I want to draw attention to the dominant emphases of thinking about 'liveness' within theatre and performance studies. In this tradition, physical co-presence is the key component, and technologies are permissible only to the extent that they do not inhibit, even might enhance, that sense of shared physical space. To such a position, livecasts are simply a scandal. But with this go some further, untested claims that audiences gain much from a sense of the *risks* of performance – that performances

DOI: 10.1057/9781137288691

are unpredictable, might go wrong. This seems to me a strange notion. Audiences generally go just once to a performance; therefore they have no measure of what might be 'accidental' in it. Further, there are plenty of performances which are planned to be as timed, predictable and inflexible as possible (I think, for instance, of the stage adaptation of *The Lion King*). It is hard to avoid the suspicion that this emphasis on risk is a performers' imputation of what they *would like* audiences to feel.[3]

'Liveness' in television and film studies

From the 1970s on, television's capacity to bring us pictures, experiences, evidence and also of course stories 'as they are happening' aroused great suspicions. With differing degrees of strength, debates among television theorists have turned on the notion that 'liveness' is something between a commercial ploy (TV selling itself) and a deceit of the very medium (TV selling a structurally deep ideology). We can capture the strength of some of these positions through one early declaration: 'Liveness is not a fact; it is an ideology.' This assertion by Robert Vianello (1985: 26) was prompted by the rise of video, but it reflects back on the supposed 'Golden Age' of early American TV – as does another early and much-cited essay by Jane Feuer (1983). Feuer challenges optimistic accounts of early TV's glories, instead proposing that its claims to ontological difference constitute part of its very ideology. She illustrates this with an examination of the prime-time programme *Good Morning, America*. Her critique emerges from her consideration of the ways the programme manages the studio host's relationship with the various feeds, giving an 'illusion' of co-presence. This she calls the programme's 'sleight-of-hand' (1983: 18) concealing its mediating role. It is out of such details for her that television's ideological role arises.[4]

In these debates relating to television, it seems that each new development stimulates theorists to ponder anew – usually pessimistically – the cultural dangers attending its claims of 'liveness'. For Vianello, it was the emergence of video. For later critics, it could be, for example, the rise of CNN, 24-hour news, and their use in the Gulf War.[5] That sense of a running tension between commerce and medium, between profits and ideology, is sustained. With television, there has been no single stellar figure whose views on 'liveness' have dominated debates. However, a substantial tradition of discussions seems to begin with John Ellis's still influential *Visible Fictions* (1982), a book which sets out to offer near-ontological

DOI: 10.1057/9781137288691

accounts of the differences between cinema and television, veering close at times to technological determinism. Ellis works through a list of defining properties of television: its intimacy, its segmentation and flow, its fugitive nature producing, he argues, a viewer's relationship of 'glancing' as opposed to 'gazing'. After discussing TV's aesthetic tendencies towards close-ups and emphasis on sound, he writes:

> However, this is to compare the broadcast TV image with the cinema image. The TV image has further distinct qualities of its own, no doubt the result of a tenacious ideological operation, that mark it decisively as different from the cinema image with its photo effect. The broadcast TV image has the effect of immediacy. It is as though the TV image is a 'live' image, transmitted and received in the same moment as it is produced. (1982: 132)

This false notion 'haunts the medium' (1982: 133), producing a simulation of conversation with viewers and a deceitful opposite to cinema's 'fully developed regime of voyeurism' (1982: 139) which trap TV's audience into 'commonsense' ideas about family, nation, class, sex and race – constituting a 'complicity of viewing' (1982: 163). This is powerful stuff.

It has not always been this way, of course. Charles Barr, in a provocative 1996 essay, argues that the dominant historiography of television has conveniently forgotten that for a considerable early period television was in fact celebrated for its liveness. He quotes many commentators, both industry and critics, arguing that this liveness was the distinguishing feature of the medium, its point of sale. So, John K. Newnham, writing in 1948, argued thus: 'There you have the strongest appeal of television. It is life while it is happening. That is why it is wrong to associate it with the cinema. It is a different medium entirely, although much of the presentation technique may be similar to that of films' (quoted by Barr, 1996: 51). Barr tracks the flow of technological innovations (such as telecine, cutting between cameras, recording and ultimately editing, on videotape) which gradually reduced the gap between television and cinema. His point is ultimately an aesthetic one, that one of the qualities to be valued in television is its capacity to convey a sense of 'liveness'. And Barr argues that this is continuing even today in at least some important examples (he cites among others Alan Bennett's 'Talking Heads' series of dramas). His concern is that a dominant hostility to televisual 'liveness' devalues such possibilities.

Another contribution to the debate travels in markedly different directions. Arising from the 1992 Manchester Broadcasting Symposium, which brought together broadcasters, critics and academics (and some spanning

DOI: 10.1057/9781137288691

these roles), *It's Live – But Is It Real?* debated the intersections between 'liveness', 'reality' and 'authenticity'. The debates covered news, music, sports coverage and war reporting – with the added spice of the symposium taking place simultaneously with that year's general election in the UK, so there was 'live' debate on coverage of that (see Miller and Allen, 1993).

Three things in particular emerge. First, there is much evidence of television's *planning for liveness*. Liveness rarely if ever just occurs in front of the camera; it is managed – not least for fear of losing control (there is a delightful account, by the director, of the problems faced in filming the 1990 Eurovision Song Contest in Zagreb). This story points the second feature, the diversity of interests at play, pushing for attention (from musicians using their participation in the live Nelson Mandela concert to reposition themselves, to television differentiating itself from the press by the way it can show up politicians' 'photo-opportunities'). All these interests help shape how live events are able to appear. But this in turn points up the third feature to emerge from the Manchester debates: the sheer diversity of kinds of liveness. A partial list of these would have to include getting behind managed façades, experiencing the risks, seeing the authentic performance, watching outcomes emerge, 'being there' for world events and gaining privileged insight into an event. Each of these drives presentations differently. Even the most troubling – CNN's coverage of the Gulf War, perhaps, with its emphasis on 'firework displays' and avoidance of analysis or investigation – is argued to be motivated less by any ideological position than by that company's drive to carve out its competitive space. All this shifts the focus away from any overarching, normative definition of liveness *per se*, towards attention to detailed circumstances.[6]

There is one other interesting opposite to the dominant negative account. It became popular in the 1990s to suggest that CNN's continuous news coverage, with its dramatic pictorial emphasis, was coming to play an independent role in pushing political actions. This idea was mooted in relation to military operations in northern Iraq (1991), Somalia (1992), Bosnia (1995) and Rwanda (post-1994). In the first three cases, the vivid, continuous televised images of suffering were said to have pushed policy-makers to intervene, perhaps because of concerns about their impact on public opinion. The Rwanda case was different. There, more complicatedly, it was suggested that the decision not to intervene militarily was a result of television's dominant presentation of Rwanda as 'far away', with unrecognisable people, who were probably fighting traditional tribal wars. But overall, the 'CNN Effect' still involved

DOI: 10.1057/9781137288691

claims that 'live and continuous imaging' had its own effects, but here these were humanitarian rather than harmful. Unusually, in this case the claims have been substantially tested. Evaluating them from a policy science perspective, Piers Robinson (2002) drew on the best evidence available on the processes and timings of policy decisions to argue that, except in very limited ways (where policy-makers themselves were very uncertain), the claimed effects are better explained by other geopolitical forces. For example, in the Iraq case, there are strong reasons to think that America was motivated by its wish to be seen to be helping Turkey, which feared an inflow of Kurdish refugees.

These exceptions aside, television studies generally distrusts 'liveness', seeing it as a false construct, a pretence by programme makers. Mapping this distrust onto livecasts would have to lead us to say that, inasmuch as the camerawork seeks to be invisible, it is deceitful. In this, curiously, television studies, with its apparently opposite account, ends up looking very like theatre and performance studies. It is, I think, helpful to look at one of the most interesting recent contributions to this area in this light. Stephanie Marriott (2007) rejects accounts of liveness as an ontological quality of the medium. She is instead interested in the ways in which television constructs experiences for audiences under the label of 'live'. Thus, it is important that presenters often go out of their way to *signal* liveness – telling us that something is immediate, that we are seeing it as it happens, and so on. This makes it possible for Marriott to track changes over time in the ways such constructing is done. She compares the coverage of John Kennedy's assassination with the coverage of the attack on the Twin Towers. In the earlier case, presenters were limited largely to passing on other people's information about what had happened (caught in phrases such as 'We are hearing that…'). In the later case, presenters wanted us to be *witnesses* to the events. We were *shown* the unfolding of the attacks and their aftermath (endlessly captured in phrases such as 'You are now seeing…'). Her account, then, discovers great complexities. Thus, discussing the BBC's coverage of the 1997 general election, Marriott shows the complicated ways in which broadcasters *staged* liveness, by for instance 'pairing' the coverage of each result with a reaction shot of one of the main political players – who had, of course, to be put in a position to monitor that very result as it came in. This was a clear way of manufacturing a particular kind of liveness.

Yet having made her account delightfully complex, when she tackles how this might *matter* Marriott seems to slip back into 'suspicion'. Writing

DOI: 10.1057/9781137288691

of television's coverage of the 2005 London police shooting of Jean Charles de Menezes, she considers the emphasis on getting witness accounts, and describes it, with Lewis et al. (2005), as 'appearance preceding substance', because investigation and explanation are 'marginalised'. Once again, 'liveness' is seen to be closing out other ways of thinking.

Debates within television studies about 'liveness' have been easily the most extensive, and are still on-going.[7] But – with rare exceptions, such as Piers Robinson – participants seem happy to speculate about harm to 'the audience' without doing research into *actual* audiences.

'Liveness' in film studies

The issue of 'liveness' arises within mainstream film theory primarily as something impossible to conceive.[8] Consider one book, near-contemporaneous with John Ellis's *Visible Fictions*, which sets out to establish the essential nature of film: James Monaco's *How to Read a Film* (1977).[9] Monaco has nothing to say about any essential differences between cinema and television. Instead, and with an eye to their potentials as *art* media, he addresses the relations between cinema and theatre. Theatre, he insists, is distinguished by being live – and this is without exploration or explanation taken to be an advantage (1977: 30). The discussion of theatre is posed in terms of the differences between Antonin Artaud's confrontational theory of theatre (use liveness to challenge and disturb your audience) and Bertolt Brecht's distanciating approach (liveness may overwhelm people's critical capacities – make space for thought). But with that benefit of liveness, for Monaco, goes yet another unargued – and again I think, simply untrue – assertion of a 'most salient' distinction between theatre and cinema: 'We watch a play as we will; we see a film only as a filmmaker wants us to see it' (1977: 33). To assert that of cinema is, first, to presume that films put no demands on audiences to choose, link and organise an understanding of the relations among things shown (their mise en scène). It also denies audiences' capacity to move within, and even beyond, the frame of the screen.[10] From such broad claims emerge the endless claims and theorisations of 'cinema spectatorship' (on this generally, see Barker, 2012).

The unfortunate results of this can be seen in the slippage which occurs in the first piece of published work on livecasts to appear. Paul Heyer's (2008) essay on the NY Met performances tells the story of the

DOI: 10.1057/9781137288691

rise of the events well, but towards the end Heyer suddenly overlays a piece of very standard film theory: the notion that cinema audiences are entrapped by the medium into a spectatorial 'voyeurism'. He writes:

> Citing film theorist Christian Metz, Ellis re-emphasizes how cinema viewing takes place in the dark, as a dream-like fantasy experience. Also, given cinema's invitation to the gaze, voyeurism is an aspect of the way we respond to the medium. These conventions also apply to DBC [digital broadcast cinema]. Close-ups can render the performers larger than life, as if on a movie screen. The gaze is crucial, since attention is usually riveted on the performers, especially in productions such as Gounod's *Roméo et Juliette* (December 15, 2007) where the two leads were riveted on each other. The tenets of voyeurism and its associated pleasures as elaborated in film theory inspired by psychoanalysis... likewise have applicability. (2008: 599).

Cinema studies have from their formation been pretty much overwhelmed by an unquestioning acceptance that cinema cannot be in any significant sense live.

In one sidewater of cinema theory, and one which intimately concerns livecasting, the issue of 'liveness' does crop up. This is Shakespeare cinema studies. This subfield is large, and attracts stellar contributions. One such, which reveals the way normative judgements operate, comes from the highly respected Catherine Belsey (1983). Belsey critiques a loss of interpretive 'openness' in film, relative to theatre. This arises, she argues, immediately from cinema's fixed viewing positions when compared with Shakespearian theatre's original almost-four-sided audience attention (which meant that actors' 'hidden' actions and facial responses would always be visible to some). Belsey goes so far as to suggest that this is part of a historical drift towards ideological control of audiences' perspectives, moving from (good, free, democratic) four-sided theatres through contained stages, to proscenium arches, contested stages, and to cinema's (bad, controlled, ideological) 'front-view' presentations.

Her argument goes beyond simply *preferring* stage presentations. She holds the formal properties of film against it. It is worth identifying two questionable moves upon which Belsey's argument depends. First, she simply assumes that *seeing from* a singular point of view (although, of course, cameras are capable of examining action from all and multiple angles) equates with *passively taking that as a given whole* (as opposed, say, to moving one's attention within and across elements, to build an account of and response to what is happening). This leads, in her

DOI: 10.1057/9781137288691

argument, to spectators thus being *prone to accept an already structured interpretation.* This very mechanistic view of the relationship between vision and cognition combines with another, less visible assumption. Belsey sees historical audiences for Shakespeare in their near-theatre-in-the-round as collectives – otherwise she would need to say that each person will have his or her 'fixed perspective' on the stage from where he or she happens to be sitting or standing. Contemporary film audiences, by contrast, are regarded as isolated, unable to see – and therefore unlikely to think – beyond the 'forced perspective' which the camerawork constructs.

Take away her particular normative judgement, and what Belsey has done is not much different from what has been argued by many film scholars, who presume that 'the spectator's' response can be derived from close formal analysis of films and cinema. Livecasting, by its nature, throws down a gauntlet to this persistent strand of theory.

'Liveness' in music studies

The issue of 'liveness' has been present in a minor key within some branches of music studies – but, strikingly, not in anything like the fashion that it has been in theatre and performance fields. Perhaps the most important difference is the simple absence of that valuation of 'risk', or the sense that the audience might shape a performance. In fact, if anything, considerations of music performance want to emphasise the *perfect professionalism* of performers – that a good performance is one which is so rehearsed, so studied, that it attains perfect embodiment. Beyond this, the main concerns here about 'liveness' have to do with defence of jobs and loss of opportunities for public performance – as in the UK Musicians' Union campaign to 'Keep It Live' (see, for instance, Frith, 2007).

There are two rare exceptions. One is John Croft's (2007) 'Theses on Liveness'. Croft is primarily concerned with the role played by electronic enhancement *in the moment of performance* and the ways in which this can reduce listeners' sense of the music having been fully produced by human beings. This relates not only to the miking of instruments, but also, for example, to the potential artistic role of the sound mixer – and it extends relentlessly to the rise of the laptop artist who generates music entirely through electronic means. What can count as authentic 'liveness' in such situations? What can count as 'virtuosity', and the 'grain' of performance

DOI: 10.1057/9781137288691

that a virtuoso adds to their performance? Therefore, for Croft, 'the "live-ness" that I'm describing would still apply in a sense to a recording of the piece, since the issue at stake is the authentic sense… of the personality of the performer'.[11] Croft identifies a fundamental historical split between those composers seeking ideal acousmatic conditions for their music and those emphasising the musician's performing body (epitomised in the solo performance). For Croft, drawing on Fredric Jameson's critique of postmodernism, the defence of 'live performance' may be charged with the task of putting bodies back into cultural history – even though he ends with a rather pessimistic note on whether this will ever work.

The other exception in music studies is Lucy Bennett's (2011) work on audiences listening at concerts. Bennett is interested in the ways in which people attending live concerts will use social media such as Twitter, and more recent phone apps such as SuperGlued, Flowd and Foursquare, to share their experiences with friends, perhaps all over the world. She sees how these developments challenge Auslander's account, 'suggesting that social media and mobile internet are now being used in an effort to blur the boundaries between those who are physically present and those who are remotely located' (2011: 12). These developments allow non-attenders to get excited before a concert as though they were getting ready to attend, and to hear and evaluate performances. The result is a substantial shift in the meanings of 'being there live'. This is a rare and important attempt to explore actual audience practices, but also astute in its understanding of specific social-technological developments.

If there is little to show in music studies in general, the specific field of opera studies offers more. Marcia Citron's 2000 study usefully digests the existing literature. Her book, which provides a substantial and complex history of opera–film relations, also acknowledges how powerfully *political* the issues here have been seen to be. On the 'left', Jeremy Tambling (1987) was interested primarily in opera's ideological constructions. On the traditionalist side, Sam Abel (1996) defended the value of liveness. But no matter their side, all opera scholars are intensely aware of the potential charge of elitism – that opera is highbrow culture at its most arch; and even when they celebrate opera, scholars want to show the ways in which it has historically taken up critical stances. But what is most striking about Citron's own position is her insistence on the difference made by the involvement of *music*: 'Screen treatments of opera can be (and have been) explored from a variety of perspectives. But we need to remember that opera *is* musical drama, and to ignore music in a major

DOI: 10.1057/9781137288691

study of media treatments is to distort the meanings of these fascinating cultural products' (2000: 3–4, emphasis in original). Music for her ensures that opera always transcends the purely political. But, curiously, this puts Citron in an awkward middle-ground, wanting to argue for the value of both live originals and screened adaptations. In effect she wants to see a distinctive new language for opera on screen with new critical criteria.[12]

This complicated ambition is made more so by her borrowings from the ontological ends of film and television theory, notably John Ellis's early work. She writes: 'With a small screen and domestic venue, television promotes familiarity and intimacy. While cinema dominates and overwhelms the viewer, television creates an environment in which the viewer can identify with the narrative on a more equal footing' (2000: 15). The melange is very difficult to work with.

But perhaps the most interesting thing to emerge comes through her discussion of a 1992 Italian experiment. A specially designed filmed performance of *Tosca* was transmitted live to cinemas across Europe, with the orchestra recorded separately at a distance in order to allow unrestrained camera access to the performance. The wish to use external light conditions to emphasise its 'live filming' meant that performers had to stay awake overnight, to film the last part at dawn, and, for Citron, this experiment had 'fascinating implications':

> This *Tosca* stresses liveness in other ways. At the start and between acts we see Rome from a helicopter whose noise is so loud that we must be inside the craft. This suggests *reportage* as in a live news report. ... Three magnificent locations – church, villa, and castle – exalt the eternal city as a mecca of civilisation. In addition, the global reach of the 'live' telecast takes on the worldly significance of the Olympics or some other international meet. And at the heart of this munificence stands Rome, and by extension Italy, the birthplace of opera. (2000: 65)

This is a wholly different vision of 'liveness' from that which we have met in other fields. It is in effect the *manufacture of togetherness*, and not limited by physical co-presence but by linking the marks of actuality with a sense of linkage to the wider world. Fascinating in itself, it has a further surprising consequence. On this approach, 'risk' becomes once again important, but as something *to be avoided at all costs*. Discussing the need for cameras not to intrude on the experience of a house audience, Citron says: 'A costly endeavour, the relay has welcomed the support of record companies, who create a video version of the telecast. But since video creates a permanent document, there is a desire for high quality in production and

DOI: 10.1057/9781137288691

performance. Live performance, however, carries the potential for error; a delayed broadcast provides an opportunity for correction and improvement' (2000: 86). Risk of error has here moved decisively from positive to negative.

Citron's influence is visible in the one direct commentary on livecasts that I have located within opera scholarship: Anthony Sheppard's (2007) long and thoughtful review of the New York Met's productions, drawing on his own very different experiences of watching Tan Dun's *The First Emperor*, first at the Met, then at a cinema. Sheppard declares that he went to the first with high hopes, but came away somewhat let down, while the second began with little sense of occasion, but then blossomed. The thing that makes the difference for him is, as for Citron, a sense of occasion, of audience collectivity, of ritual. But these have to come to life. Going to the opera for Sheppard involves dressing up; therefore the cinema had to fight its way up, as he went in jeans. But it also involves having 'wow' responses to spectacle, and the cinema magnified these. Together, these should generate collective celebration: clapping, cheering, a 'general frenzy'.

Sheppard takes from Citron an optimism about the future of these kinds of event, even through the notion that livecast audiences will learn to 'identify with the theatre audience' by glimpsing them at various points. Whatever the value of this particular notion, it does seem that opera scholarship has largely escaped the textual pessimism to which theatre studies has been particularly prone. Operas are libretti waiting to be embodied and come to life. Alive, they are large, ebullient forms for us to drown ourselves in, collectively – whether at the opera house or at the cinema.

'Liveness' in virtual performance studies

At a far extreme from other approaches is the recent emergence of the field of virtual performance research. With strong industry links, this research world is interested in asking when, and why, we feel close to people via technologies – and how this sense of closeness might be enhanced.[13] So, how might mobile phones, or the internet, or particular web platforms be designed to bridge physical gaps? Several journals, often closely associated with the cognitive and brain sciences, have emerged in this field: *Presence*, for instance, and *Virtual Environments*. In this kind of thinking, physical co-presence is something that can be artificially created. Clear examples of the directions it has taken can be

DOI: 10.1057/9781137288691

gleaned from the articles in recent issues of *Presence*. Here is to be found talk of how 'a more natural user interface between the player and the game world can create a more immersive, realistic, and fun experience for the player' (Shafer et al., 2011), of how 'perceived video game realism is a predictor of spatial presence and enjoyment' (McGloin et al., 2011), and – most overtly – of how 'augmented reality technologies' can 'be used to manipulate beliefs and perceptions and alter the reported experience of pain' (Regenbrecht et al., 2011). This is clearly *interventionist* research.

In a related vein, a number of performance artists have begun to exploit advanced technologies for creating, storing and transmitting their work, trying out new modes of interactivity in the process. An example would be Camille Baker's MINDtouch project, which explored 'how and whether liveness and presence could be sensed during ... mobile social events' (2011: 100).[14] This, of course, is a fundamental challenge to those still heavily invested in ideas of direct physical presence, and the resultant theorisations via ideas such as 'the extended body' show many signs of conceptual effort and difficulty.[15]

A troubling implication emerges from Baker's research, that technologies might be most effective where they are least perfect. Baker celebrates imperfections, or what she calls 'graininess', which she argues might enhance a sense of 'real presence'. My suspicion is that while this might work with things we don't recognise or feel we know – too perfect an image might make us think of adverts, for instance – the whole point for audiences of livecasting appears to be its capacity to be invisible as technology. Enthusiastic audiences for a livecast don't want to be reminded of the fact that it is being transmitted. One of the commonest complaints in my questionnaire responses concerned blips in transmission, which disrupt concentrated participation. And in this assertion, Baker clearly stands apart from the more overtly persuasion-driven American researchers whom I cited above, for whom technological transparency is pretty clearly a precondition of influence.

Whatever the undoubted interest and value in this field of research, it is clearly a mile away from all the other approaches in its understanding of 'liveness'.

'Liveness' in comedy studies

Smaller debates about 'liveness' have taken place in some other, surprising fields. One such discussion, within comedy studies, is worth attention.

DOI: 10.1057/9781137288691

Jason Rutter (1997) and Fabiola Scarpetta and Anna Spagnolli (2009) explore how stand-up comedians generate, through their acts, convincing senses of 'locality' for their audiences. Drawing on the traditions and concerns of conversation analysis, they point out how frequently comedians open with comments about the town and the venue, how they pick out audience members to be butts of carefully toned jokes which pick up on local peculiarities and how thereby they generate specific senses of occasion and participation for their house audiences, who will still understand that they are getting an otherwise set routine that might have been touring for a long time. This emphasis on the need to *create* presence is unusual, since it suggests that 'liveness' can be as much about belonging to a locality and community as about physical presence *per se*. And in that sense these studies' roots in conversation analysis become important; conversation analysis puts central emphasis on the *work* which speakers have to do to open and then maintain channels, and the fact that therefore communication is an *achievement*. For this reason, Rutter talks extensively about 'the construction of liveness' as a component of stand-up comedians' work.

This research has so far limited itself to the performers' work in trying to create that sense. I would be interested to see how this might be extended to take account of televised recordings of such local performances, for instance, or DVD sets of comedians' tours. In a passing comment, Rutter seems almost to dismiss this possibility, remarking that these modes of constructing liveness are 'not relevant to broadcast performances' (1997: 193). In my (admittedly limited) experience of recordings of touring stand-up performances, this is not obviously true.

'Liveness' in sports studies

A final – and very different – set of considerations about 'liveness' emerges from sports sociology. There, television's increasing role in creating global audiences for sports such as football, cricket and rugby, and massive coverage of specific events such as the Olympics and the World Cup, has produced a growing body of work on how fans engage with events at a distance, including in collective contexts such as pubs with large screens. A number of scholars have looked at the rise of live transmissions of football (and other) matches to public contexts such as pubs, or to large-screen presentations away from the game itself.

Mike Weed (2007) draws on the work of John Urry (2002), who distinguishes three types of proximity at work in contemporary culture:

DOI: 10.1057/9781137288691

face-to-face, face-the-place and face-the-moment. Weed uses this catego-
risation to depict the ways in which pubs, especially when they become
regular venues, become a kind of surrogate live space – with the bonus
that they can partly recreate the old, now forbidden pleasures of the football terrace (risky jokes, uncensored chanting and the like). And for key
events, this participation can gain even more credibility when the media
start, in turn, reporting on fans' responses in pubs. A circuit emerges in
which fans' responses gain further validation by being counted as part of
the event. Weed also (2010) examines the parallel phenomenon of fans
going to World Cup games without tickets, in the hope of an experience
of 'being there' – and how in some cases this has been catered to by large-
screen showings of the match outside the stadium. His summary sentence,
'the need for proximity is to the experience rather than the game' (2010:
411), well captures the force of this whole approach.

Garry Whannel and John Horne (2008) put a historical perspective
on this, looking at the long association between football, male bonding
and beer (much of their argument is about the branding of beers, and
the links to sports sponsorship). After the bad times in the UK of 1970s
hooliganism, the Bradford City fire and the Hillsborough deaths came
the Taylor Report on all-seater stadia and the rise of the Premier League.
This shifted the professional game in major ways, and increasingly
divorced it from working-class culture. Whannel and Horne argue that
the rise of pub viewing became part of a reclaiming of the game: 'it is in
the pub, more than in the de-classed environs of the stadium, that the
old alliance of beer, men and football has been re-forged' (2008: 62).

In the same volume, Garry Crawford elaborates this argument, exploring
the history of alcohol in relation to sports and the ways in which the disin-
hibition magnifies the sports event. The emergence of sports scenes – sites
where people can gather to participate without physical presence – has
produced a new kind of exceptional event, he argues: 'what is significant
and similar about all of these locations, be that a sport stadium, pub or
bar, open-air space in front of a big screen, or someone's home, is the
creation and sense of "place" that makes these "extraordinary", and that
this is achieved through (often alcohol enhanced) social performances
(and in turn audiencing) within these locations' (2008: 281). They are, in
other words, their own *kinds* of event, with their own rules, expectations
and requirements.

The sociological orientation underpinning this work results in a very
different picture and conceptualisation from those of either theatre and

DOI: 10.1057/9781137288691

performance or television studies. Here, a key question is how and to what extent people generate a cultural context which they can then *own* and thus *treat as 'live'*. Clearly, the creation of regular working-class spaces for collective watching of matches is a strong case. The differences from the much more middle-class, and temporary, appropriation of cinema spaces for special cultural screenings are great. But they do not negate the value of asking the questions this way.

What does this (incomplete) survey of debates indicate? First, there is a mass and, I would suggest, a mess of largely separate and irreconcilable ideas about the meaning and implications of 'liveness'. Most are purely theoretical, neither based upon nor tested by empirical investigations. Instead, they often grow out of claims about the supposed special nature of a cultural form or medium. Second, claims about the role of 'liveness' look frequently like disguised normatives – they are written as descriptive, but are actually assertions of what critics either want or don't want to happen. And it seems that the more speculative they are, the more they are used as the basis for quality and value judgements. 'Liveness' matters greatly to most who discuss it; it is something to be *concerned about*. Third, they are almost all written entirely from the points of view of producers and distributors, with a real absence of attention to the ways audiences might *experience* liveness.[16] The one exception to this is within sports studies, and especially the sociological work on football fans in pubs.

We can perhaps distinguish a series of dimensions to 'liveness' which are differently conceived and valued by the various traditions. Almost all the approaches presume the importance of *simultaneity*. Only music studies, to a degree, addresses the possibilities of captured and recorded liveness. *Bodily co-presence* with performers is the *sine qua non* for theatre and performance studies, but is not an issue for sports researchers, for whom watchers' co-presence generates its own special dynamic – or indeed for opera researchers. We might say that a new notion is emerging from this, which we could call *eventness*: that is, the creation of and participation in senses of heightened cultural togetherness. *Experienced risk* – that the performance is not 'locked', and might be shaped by the audience's responses – is again desired by theatre and performance scholars, and is also loved by sports fans – for whom there is a kind of lived collective illusion of influence at a distance. *Immediacy* – which itself encompasses several dimensions, but all focused around the audience's power to decide how to watch – matters not at all to sports scholarship, for which the close-up and

DOI: 10.1057/9781137288691

(repeated) slow-motion replay are just givens, but matters hugely to many theatre scholars, for whom the camera's intervention is an invasion and control of free perception. To most television studies, this is the very thing which proves 'liveness' to be almost fraudulent. A *sense of place and locality* matters to comedy scholars, but is something that needs to be achieved; it is taken for granted by sports scholars (the stadium's 'holy ground'). It is a sort of active factor for opera scholars (the physical setting contributes a distinctive shaping to the rituals of engagement), but is largely ignored in theatre thinking. All approaches presume a *ready and prepared audience*, but understand different things by this. For sports, comedy and opera, it is the willingness to join the rituals of the game enthusiastically. For theatre and performance, it is more the right kind of attentiveness.

The oddball among all these is the recently emerged virtual performance studies, with their focus on 'presence'. For this field, it seems, all the above are up for grabs. 'Liveness' is not a descriptive or normative concept, but a *tool* and a *goal*. Its question appears to be not whether liveness is present, but how can we make people *feel* that it is? Its heart is in the persistent tradition of American persuasion research.

This cacophony of contradictory claims and theories begins to look mildly absurd when we consider the ways in which livecasts breach all boundaries. Here are theatrical, operatic, dance, musical, comedic, sporting and other performances taken from their source-point, captured by digital technologies and by aesthetic practices owing most to television outside broadcasts. They are transmitted to cinemas, amid the assemblage of expectations that go with such spaces, and displayed on large screens with attendant surround-sound ambience. New senses of locality (the auditorium, the venue, recurrent audiences) are involved. Audiences know this is different. The presentations emphasise the difference, in a dozen ways. The emergence of livecasts, with all these crossovers, pretty evidently invites researchers to step out of their separate domains and think more self-critically about their investments in 'liveness'. To date, that has hardly happened.[17] In the next chapter, I summarise what my research revealed about how livecasts' audiences understand and feel about the issue of 'liveness' in these events.

Notes

1   My thanks to Alastair Oatey at Picturehouse for allowing me to see this unpublished research.

DOI: 10.1057/9781137288691

2   See, for instance, Erika Fischer-Lichte (2008) and Matthew Reason (2006),
    who astutely identifies how nervous adherents of liveness become over
    documentation of their performances.

3   I don't wish to deny that there can be real pleasures associated with the
    unexpected in performances. An especially illuminating example is given by
    Penelope Woods in her PhD thesis on audiences at the open-roofed Globe
    Theatre in London. At one performance of *Macbeth* in 2010, a pigeon landed
    on the stage as actor Jasper Britton was about to deliver the famous speech
    'Life's but a walking shadow, a poor player that struts and frets his hour upon
    the stage'. Pausing, he fixed the pigeon with a gaze, spoke the lines – and
    then waited until the bird flew off, before ending ' … and then is heard no
    more'. The story is marvellous in itself, but has the virtue of throwing light
    on the complexity of what is meant by 'being there'. What counts as the
    reception environment cannot be predetermined. In principle, of course, this
    unexpected addition could have been appreciated just as much if this had
    been livecast, since its unpredictability would surely have remained visible
    (see Woods, 2007: 251–2).

4   It is interesting to read Feuer's guarded protestation, no doubt prompted
    by her awareness of David Morley's *The Nationwide Audience*, that she was
    willing to submit her claims to empirical testing. I say 'guarded' because
    by the end of her statement of this, she says in effect that she isn't sure
    there is anything that *could* be tested, such is the virtual invisibility of the
    phenomenon she is depicting.

5   A very good summary of many of the tensions around this is contained in
    Brent McGregor's 1997 book.

6   For a recent argument along the same lines, see Ytreberg (2006).

7   For a soon-to-be-published major re-evaluation, see Scannell (2012).

8   There have been one or two minor streams of thought about films which go
    in other directions. Most notably, there has been a current of interest in the
    concept of 'ostension' – that is, that we need to pay attention to the *simple
    showing* that films achieve. In the work of those who study pornography,
    the simple 'showing' of bodies and sex is powerful and significant (Linda
    Williams' notion of the 'frenzy of the visible' is a good example; see
    Williams, 2009). There is also a minor but persistent interest in the idea that
    films can be seen to *enact* things in front of us (see, for instance,
    Koven, 2008). This has also been present in the work of some star scholars
    who have addressed the idea of being able, in films, to see the star through
    and behind their performances (see, for instance, Drake, 2006; Bode,
    2010).

9   Monaco's title indicates his intended sweeping scope. Interestingly, although
    many other parts of his book changed in later editions, I could detect no
    changes or elaborations in the parts I consider here.

DOI: 10.1057/9781137288691

10   The concept of 'off-screen space' emerged in the 1970s as scholars explored
     the operation of mise en scène within films. It references the many ways in
     which action on screen can point beyond the boundaries of the visible – by
     characters' looks, by noises off, by implied presence (shadows, shifts in
     lighting, etc.), by 'owned' point of view shots and the like.

11   John Croft, personal email, 2010.

12   This search for an emergent form shows particularly clearly within her telling
     of the history of opera on screen when she writes of *The Medium* (1951) that its
     transformation from stage to screen, accomplished with the addition of extra
     music, amounted to the creation of a 'truly new opera for the screen, tailored
     specifically for the medium ... a new work for cinema' (Citron, 2000: 38).

13   For an example of this kind of applied research, see Shin and Shin (2011).
     Here, 'presence' is something to be artificially achieved, in order to ease and
     encourage consumption.

14   See also Daniel Palmer (2000), who reflects on the slice-of-life webcams
     initiated by 'Jenniecam' and considers their possibilities as the basis for
     artworks which might simultaneously use and critique their promises of
     immediacy and 'authenticity'.

15   See, for instance, Susan Kozel's almost impenetrable reworking of Merleau-
     Ponty in her *Closer* (2008).

16   A particularly clear example of this occurs in an essay on dance and 'liveness'.
     Its authors, Ivani Santana and Fernando Iazzetta (n.d.), propose a variation
     on Auslander's model based on analysing their own dance production.

17   It is interesting to note that some years before the emergence of these
     high-culture streamed events, suppliers were already talking of the likely
     differences that might need to be considered. In 2002, *Screen Daily* carried
     a report on forthcoming developments: ' "You have to figure out who
     you're going to attract in to what type of alternative content," said Wendy
     Aylsworth, vice president technology, Warner Bros. Technical Operation.
     "When you go to see a motion picture, you're expecting to get absorbed
     into that setting – the sound and the image is the focal point. In some of
     the other alternatives that's not what the whole experience is about – there's
     something else going on in the mind of that person and you have to cater
     for that. In a movie, you're going to be sitting quietly, getting absorbed in it.
     With alternative content, the experience is the focus." UK exhibitor UCI has
     been screening live World Cup soccer matches in some of its sites, charging
     from around Euros 15 up to Euros 60 for a corporate package. "Given the fact
     that you can go to any pub or café in England and see the matches for free,
     it's quite an achievement that we've seen significant audiences," said Gerald
     Buckle, project director of UCI UK' (Forde, 2002a). These insights have not,
     to my knowledge, been followed up in any more substantive way.

DOI: 10.1057/9781137288691

5
Livecasts' Audiences Talk about 'Liveness'

Abstract: *This chapter explores the ways in which 'liveness' is understood by livecasts' audiences. Drawing primarily on the author's own research, it shows that 'liveness' does matter greatly to many audience members, but that the meaning of 'liveness' is contested, and that different features of the presentations are valued according to audiences' proximity to either 'Expert' or 'Immersive' orientations. Five distinct dimensions of 'liveness' are identified, on each of which 'Experts' and 'Immersives' stand opposed in their preferences.*

Barker, Martin. *Live To Your Local Cinema: The Remarkable Rise of Livecasting*. Basingstoke: Palgrave Macmillan, 2013. DOI: 10.1057/9781137288691.

We have already seen that liveness is an important issue for livecasts' audiences, not least from NESTA's evidence that those attending the cinema presentations valued this as much as theatregoers. But that just re-emphasises how complex this concept must be. And, as anyone who has ever conducted audience research will attest, the moment you ask people directly, things get complicated. In this chapter I try to go beyond simply showing that people differ in their responses, to revealing a pattern to those responses. But first, it does need to be noted that people were very alive to this as an issue. This is shown by a simple measure of the length of answers to my questions. For a random sample of forty respondents across my four main open-text questions, Table 5.1 shows how the average length of answers varies.

TABLE 5.1   *Average number of words in answers to four open-ended questions*

Why have you given this rating?	26.0
Why did you go?	17.0
What disappointments if any?	36.8
The meanings of 'liveness' to you?	42.2

Source: author's data.

These longer answers to the question concerning 'liveness' come even though this was the last question in my questionnaire.

Liveness also matters in a strictly temporal sense. Recall how, in Picturehouse's research, respondents' interest in seeing a livecast fell by 50 per cent if it would be delayed by 24 hours. Some sense that it is going on now matters greatly to many people. Thinking and caring about 'liveness' is not something special to academics; it feeds into the thoughts and expectations of many attenders. One way in which this makes itself visible is in people's use of certain discursive markers. People responding to my question about 'liveness' repeatedly used a series of expressions which hint at their expectations, and their fulfilment or breach: expressions such as 'obviously', 'of course' and 'naturally' (which point towards expectations), and 'strangely', 'surprisingly' and 'weirdly' (which suggest challenges to those expectations). These expressions occurred quite often. Here are some illustrative examples (drawn from across the entire set):

> Naturally the experience of actually being in the opera house with all the Buzz and excitement cannot be reproduced. That apart, it was better than a live

DOI: 10.1057/9781137288691

performance in two respects. Having close-ups of the singers was better than using opera glasses. Secondly having cameras behind the stage in the interval was fascinating. Having the time left of the interval on the screen was another bonus. [483]

Obviously not the atmosphere of being at the theatre, but the interviews and behind scenes shots made up for it. [581]

Obviously lacks the every night an event feel – but the directed camera actually adds to emotional impact. I think this is a really valuable addition to the availability of arts. [357]

You actually get a better view of the performance than in the actual theatre. The sound is always excellent. Obviously the atmosphere is not the same although the audience do often respond with applause. [344]

Of course a streamed performance cannot compare with a live performance. However in some opera houses – notably Covent Garden – unless you have paid the earth you don't always have an uninterrupted view of the stage. This is not the case in a streamed performance. For me, not better or worse, but different. [479]

The common component in all these is the acceptance that a streamed cinematic presentation is bound to lack some component of 'liveness', which is so obvious that it hardly needs saying – but whose precise significance therefore becomes oddly fugitive. There are, of course, mixed feelings about what might be emerging in its place, and how attractive the qualities of this might be. But in particular, those who use indicative expressions such as 'surprising' and 'strangely' seem to be moving – tentatively, perhaps – towards expressing the nature of the emergent experience for them:

Larger than life...surprisingly intimate, great visibility, and interesting introductions. [550]

Strangely more absorbing, because camera operator expertise presents a huge variety of shots and engages the concentration more deeply in the performance. [20]

Better because you're practically there on stage with the singers rather than seeing them from some distance in a live theatre. You do however miss the immediate excitement of a live performance and being in the presence of great artists, but surprisingly this is no big deal. [285]

It's better than any seat in the house. The only slightly weird thing is that everyone feels they want to applaud the best things but it is silly to applaud a cinema screen. [288]

DOI: 10.1057/9781137288691

To me, these comments suggest that the expectations, conventions and 'manners' of livecasts are still forming, and the difference that they will make in the longer term to people's perceptions and hopes cannot yet be known. But there are some among the respondents for whom this was, in effect, a new kind of cultural experience. It might have its *own form of liveness* for them:

> Having attended the Metropolitan Opera in New York many times (in fact I attended during one of the live broadcasts last year), I find the experience more intense and gripping at the cinema. The Met is such a huge and cavernous space that I felt very little connection with what was happening on stage. On the cinema screen, being able to see the faces of the singers and registering the emotions they convey offers a far better experience. The sound in the multiplexes is also surprisingly more vibrant and involving than a live set-up. In addition I find the UK cinema audiences at these events far more attentive and better behaved than the American audiences at the Met where talking, eating and fidgeting can prove extremely annoying. [530]

> Better, because you're practically there on stage with the singers, rather than seeing them from some distance in a live theatre. You do however miss the immediate excitement of a live performance and being in the presence of great artists, but surprisingly this is no big deal. Also I'd never be able to afford to go to a dozen operas of this quality in a season anyway, so each one is a bonus. [285]

> Better view, better price, the addition of the interesting interviews make this experience preferable. There was a feeling of liveness so much so that I wanted to clap but felt a bit silly doing so. I missed this – the opportunity to respond with applause to performers who could hear that applause. I liked the intervals with drinks just as at the event itself for the opportunity of relaxing and chatting with others about the performance in progress. [360]

With these first examples of enthusiastic adoption in mind, I turn to the ways my respondents explain their feelings about 'liveness'. As ever, the askance eye that audience research brings to preconceived theories raises awkward challenges for assumptions about livecasts, but perhaps to none more so than all those assuming theories about 'liveness'. Liveness *is* an issue for audiences at these events, but not in a singular manner. For some, it is understood in a very traditional way. Nothing can replace being there in the house. Such people really don't much like livecasts, even if they may go for want of any alternatives. But what interests me is that these traditionalists are likely to offer vernacular theorisations

DOI: 10.1057/9781137288691

of liveness in a manner which challenges some core claims of theatre scholars. As we will see, for this group liveness is much about retaining control. It is an insistence on their ability to manage their responses for themselves, not to be drawn closely into engagement. Critical distance is crucial to them.

But for those who embrace the emergent phenomenon of livecasts, liveness understood in this way is relatively unimportant. They are willing to sacrifice that for something else which they discover at these events: an experience of *privileged access*. This privilege is, of course, partly about the getting of otherwise impossible tickets, and at affordable prices. But it is also about being taken close to a performance in all its glory *and* with all its faults. It is also about a kind of cultural education, where subtitles, interviews, back-stage insights and special extras help audiences who claim no specialist knowledge to see inside. We can best understand this idea of privileged access by seeing it almost like a ladder, with lower and higher rungs. At its lowest, it is just being able to see something that would otherwise be too distant, or too expensive. This is the bottom rung. Next up might come the sense that certain physical disadvantages are removed by the cinema presentation: not being able to see or hear well, or finding theatres difficult to manage. This easily extends to a third rung: finding cinemas a more congenial environment, less precious, critical, exclusive. Add in bonuses such as subtitles, behind-the-scenes interviews, guidance from directors on what to watch and listen for, brief histories and story summaries for the uninitiated, and the livecast can feel like a way of climbing up into an otherwise closed world.

The dimensions of 'liveness'

Close analysis of people's spoken responses to these events leads me to distinguish five separable aspects of liveness, and to discern a dimension of responses for each of them. The five aspects are 'immediacy', 'intimacy', 'buzz', 'learning' and 'being (in) the audience'. Let us briefly consider each in turn:

1   *Immediacy*: this is very much bound up with the fact that the event is unfolding as it is being watched. It is fostered by any sense of being able to interact with performers or communicate responses to the event. Typical phrasings expressing this are 'sense

DOI: 10.1057/9781137288691

of risk ... there could be gaffes ... knowing it's going on ... wondering how it will go ... watching them achieve it ... wanting to clap ... wish they could hear us clap'.

2   *Intimacy*: this involves feeling close to the performers and the action, perhaps even in some sense *enabling* it to happen, by the way in which one responds. It also involves sensing how performers are achieving their performances. Typical phrasings include 'feeling you can get inside their performances ... knowing they are doing this for you ... intense emotions with the characters'.

3   *Buzz*: this involves having one's reactions heightened by the awareness that other audience members are also engaged, excited, moved, and sharing the pleasure of the performance with them. Typical phrasings include 'hearing the anticipation ... watching other people's reactions ... talking in the interval ... finding like-minded people'.

4   *Expanding oneself*: this involves knowing that one may or should go away from the performance added to, enlarged, perhaps changed by the experience. Typical phrasings include 'concentrating on the meanings ... getting to understand what they are trying to say ... picking up information from programmes, etc ... hearing things I didn't know before ... bonuses and extras'.

5   *Being (in) the audience*: this has a distinct element of self-referentiality, that one knows how to be the kind of person who knows how to respond to performances of this kind. One knows that one understands and appreciates the conventions appropriate to this kind of event. Typical phrasings include 'talking to others like me in the interval ... going with/taking/being taken by others to share ... knowing what to attend to, what to listen for, where to look'.

For each of these five aspects, there are two poles, one of which I dub 'Immersive', the other 'Expert' – these terms being intended to capture something of the relationship with the events that the different people are seeking. For example, those adopting an 'Immersive' strategy welcomed all the bonus materials, because these materials allowed them to become audiences in a way that previously they had not been able to. 'Experts', on the other hand, displayed a feeling that the event was almost being misappropriated: they see themselves as holding expertise which the livecasts undercut. Livecasts can be seen to succeed or fail according to how one interprets each of these dimensions, as I hope Table 5.2 (derived from answers within my research materials) indicates.

DOI: 10.1057/9781137288691

TABLE 5.2   *'Immersive' v. 'Expert' orientations to livecasts*

Immersives	Dimensions of 'liveness'	Experts
Being there as it is all happening, wherever that happens to be and whatever is offered.	IMMEDIACY	Being able to interact with but also critically appreciate the performance.
Getting as close as possible to the performers, in order to become intimate with them.	INTIMACY	Getting an appropriate closeness that will aid appreciation and evaluation.
Being with the right others makes it as good as being at the event.	BUZZ	'Others' have to be appropriate in that they share the right ways of responding.
Extra information boosts closeness and intimacy – giving access to performers' sense of their purposes.	LEARNING	Extra information can cloud perspective, superimposing performers' perspectives on necessary critical judgement.
Learning how to be at and part of this kind of event, and thus how to participate.	BEING (IN) THE AUDIENCE	Knowing how to call on experience and expert criteria to evaluate the overall value of the performance.

While there are differences across all five dimensions, the most striking are in people's attitudes to *learning*. 'Experts' believe strongly in forming their own judgements on the basis of knowledge which they bring to the event. 'Immersives' welcome being guided and shown. If this is right, then the difference between the source-event and its streamed version is about much more than physical co-presence.

Much of the variation can be seen in the ways people talk about their 'distance' from the event. This word gets to carry a wide range of meanings. For some, distance was a *problem* overcome by the cinema presentation. You were no longer lost in the cheap seats, far away from the event both visually and acoustically. To this is added a second dimension: the use of close-ups, which accentuates the physical work of the actors/singers. People could be ambivalent, and attracted or repelled along different dimensions, as these responses show – all in reply to my question about

DOI: 10.1057/9781137288691

the ways in which livecasts were like or unlike, and better or worse than, attending the source-event:

> Obviously you lose some of the immediacy of live theatre/opera. And close-ups of opera singers all too often dispel the mystery & magic of the story-line (too old, can't act...). And surprisingly inept camera work... But at its best you forget the distance & the fact of cinema and are caught up in the music & drama – and incredible voices. [551]

> Unlike... you get to see behind the scenes – good. Like... the music, story. Better... great comfort, plenty of leg room, not an enormous distance from the action, can see facial expressions, can take loo breaks without disturbing/distracting/annoying other people. Worse... not live music, visually shots chosen for you. [387]

> The experience is not the same as live, but very good alternative for events I cannot attend live. Advantage is close ups of singers – usually only distance views in live opera. [321]

> In the opera house you are at a fixed distance and height from the stage, at a screening both are varied, which enhances the experience. [69]

But for others, the idea of distance takes on a more metaphorical meaning, as in these responses to my question:

> There is a definite air of disembodiment that has to be overcome. Viewing a live event as part of a cinema presentation does cause one step of distance between audience and performers. Further there is no audience like a live audience which is part of the experience – otherwise you may as well buy the DVD. [4]

> There is a greater distance between yourselves and the performers. You are aware that it is a relayed performance by reason of limitations in the technology. There is no smell of the grease paint. The social conventions are different. For instance you can take drinks into the cinema to consume during the transmission. [194]

> It was a very strange mix. There was an intimacy that I usually associate with live theatre but at the same time a distance that comes with cinema. The whole audience seemed slightly ill at ease – for example was it OK to come in late or cough. Although in general it was good to have the cinematic experience some of the camera shots and the panning was quite irritating – not quite what I would have wanted to look at, at that particular moment. So you were at the mercy of the producer in a way that you aren't in either cinema or live theatre. [270]

That notion of being 'at the mercy' of others is the gateway to a wider discourse about an audience member's right to control where he or

DOI: 10.1057/9781137288691

she looks and how he or she listens. And it associates with a surprising reversal of expectations. Those who are most committed to the importance of physical co-presence are the ones who are most likely to say that they *do not like being brought too close to the performers*. This leads, they argue, to the loss of something they need if they are to have what they desire: a critical relationship. They need a certain distance to be able to sustain what they need: a clear sense of the *illusion* of the performance:

> Definitely worse except that one can take a glass of wine into the cinema. Opera is physical: you need to be there. Cinema in this form offers a false rapport which I find hypocritical and distasteful especially when plugged as it is by the Met. Sometimes the camera work obtrudes. No sense of occasion. I might like it more if it was done more to my taste. [643]

> I have mixed feelings about the add-ons – the things one gets that one wouldn't get being there. It is really interesting to see the scene shifts and the back-stage set-up in general. Some interviews can be interesting but they are dreadfully badly done – gushy and self-serving when they should be more probing. But to be so they would have been done at a different time not when the stars have just finished an aria and are preparing for the next act. Doing them that way also breaks the necessary illusion and suspension of disbelief that the performers rely to on to carry an audience through the show. [414]

> You see the singers in close-up – whether this is a good or bad thing depends on the singers! At best it really feels as if you were present. Audiences sometimes applaud. I don't myself but wish there was some way a distant audience could convey appreciation. The long intervals are inescapable. In a theatre you would not get the filler material and while it is always interesting, it totally destroys the illusion of being there. [77]

There is something striking about the insistence by 'Expert' audiences that they prefer this kind of distance that allows them to work imaginatively, and selectively, across a performance. They decline what they feel is an invitation to too close an involvement in the performance because, in this destruction of the 'necessary illusion' of the performance, they risk losing their capacity stand outside it.

Emergent manners

I believe that the opposition I have just described may help us understand how new 'manners' of participation emerge. We know from many historical examples that important changes in ways of participating in

DOI: 10.1057/9781137288691

forms of culture have taken place. In a number of cases, cultural historians have captured points of transition in modes of participating in culture, and the attendant shifts in the status of particular cultural ideas or practices. For instance, Robert Darnton (1984) has, among a number of other cases, looked at the changes in reading practices which emerged with Jean-Jacques Rousseau's works on education. James Johnson (1996) has captured a shift in the ways in which people listened attentively to music in nineteenth-century Paris. For the same period, Lawrence Levine (1990) has charted the fundamental shift in the cultural location of Shakespeare's work within America, bringing with it a major change in how his plays were attended to. These immensely valuable studies have depended, of course, on locating the scattered remnants of evidence to display shifts in ways of relating to cultural forms. The limitations of seeing these processes historically can, in principle, be overcome as we watch this phenomenon emerge, take shape and embed itself.

In the evidence I have gathered, there are many signs of this awareness among those who are inclined to be most enthusiastic that new manners will need to emerge for them to be able to take part uninhibitedly, as they wish. As respondent 360 (quoted above) put it, 'There was a feeling of liveness so much so that I wanted to clap but felt a bit silly doing so.' This is, I want to argue, a new mode of participation, not just a different space for doing so. There is much to do to understand the differences this is introducing. What we cannot afford to do is to allow prejudgements about what *ought* to happen to block our seeing what *does* happen.

The concept of 'intermediality'

In Christopher Balme's contribution to the 'liveness' debate, as we saw, the concept of 'intermediality' plays an important role. Expanding on this concept in his *Cambridge Introduction to Theatre Studies* (2008a), he distinguishes three possible meanings. There is, first, the simple transposition of content from one medium to another – something which has long been the topic of adaptation studies. Second, it can mean the general increase in levels of intertextual reference and interdependence. It is the third meaning which he regards as the most relevant. This is 'the attempt to realise in one medium the aesthetic conventions and/or patterns of seeing and hearing of another medium' (2008a: 206). Balme's distinctions are helpful. In the book, his primary exemplifications of his

DOI: 10.1057/9781137288691

third meaning are theatre groups such as The Wooster Group and The Builders' Association, who incorporate media in their performances not only as additional materials, but as expansions of their relationships with their audiences.

But these very exemplifications might be our reason for thinking that this is not quite the ground for understanding livecasts. For they still presume that in some sense audiences will persist in perceiving each medium as a distinguishable 'system' whose conventions can be separately identified and transported. Here is theatre borrowing and incorporating bits of other media. An alternative would be to see the result of such intermedial movements as the emergence of a *merged medium* with supervenient conventions and practices. And there may be mileage in this.[1] But I still do not think it captures the heart of the issue. I want, instead, to propose that we need to explore directly the *rise of new manners of participation*, to see the ways in which audiences communally produce new ways of 'doing liveness'. This takes us, in my view, inevitably to the borderlands of sociology, to consider class and community formations, to consider differentiated and historically shifting modes of participation in different media and cultural practices, and to see how people *think about themselves* in and through these. I close this chapter with a small personal example.

A few years ago, while holidaying in Wisconsin, my wife and I visited the city of Madison. We chanced on a local event. Over the summer, in the early evening one day a week, the local symphony orchestra put on live performances of popular classical music in front of City Hall. Hugely popular, these performances attract thousands of people, who camp out with picnic tables, chairs, hampers and bottles of wine. Knowing residents have developed a set of 'rules' for this. From early in the day, blankets are laid down all round the hall, to which their owners will return later and laden, with prime spaces in front of the performance area going early in the morning. Those arriving later can still hear the performance through loudspeakers all round the hall, but of course they can neither see the orchestra nor hear the music directly. We, unknowing visitors, lacked blankets, chairs, food or wine, but we chose to stay because we quite liked the live feel to the event. Anecdotes are always risky, but this situation intrigues me. One might argue that people at different points around City Hall were on a gradient of liveness – the more they could see the performers, and the closer they were to the un-amplified sound, the extra liveness they were getting. On the other

DOI: 10.1057/9781137288691

hand, the further away they were, a different kind of liveness seemed to kick in – one in which people were primarily enjoying the *occasion*. They chatted, ate, drank and behaved convivially. The music plus its free provision provided an ambience. A distinct set of 'manners' for correct behaviour had emerged. People arrived for the concert's beginning. They still applauded at the end of each piece. And they left when it ended. But what was being celebrated, I sensed, was in some senses *themselves*: citizens of Madison enjoying their sense that this was special to their city, a mark of its cultured nature – even its distinctiveness within the otherwise very rural and conservative Wisconsin. They were *living* this mark of their city's distinctive nature. Thinking about the liveness of such events in this way would entail a wholesale re-theorisation of what we mean and intend by the concept.

Note

1   In an email exchange, Paul Heyer told me one interesting fact about the New York Met livecasts. Aware of the impact of introducing close-ups of performers, they had begun using Hollywood-experienced make-up artists to get performers camera-ready. This is one small indicator of the realisation of audience expectations arising from merging the media.

DOI: 10.1057/9781137288691

6
The Cultural Status of Livecasts

Abstract: *Examining the challenges posed by livecasting to ideas about the social value of arts and culture, this chapter relates these to on-going debates around the work of Pierre Bourdieu, and his thesis that cultural tastes are hierarchically organised and connected to perceptions both of value and of class position. It identifies, instead, some appeals to notions of 'democratisation of the arts' that work rhetorically to justify changes in the funding and provision of the arts that arise from other processes.*

Barker, Martin. *Live To Your Local Cinema: The Remarkable Rise of Livecasting.* Basingstoke: Palgrave Macmillan, 2013. DOI: 10.1057/9781137288691.

Consider the following quotes from enthusiasts within my research:

> Judging by the demand for opera and for the National Theatre's production of Phèdre in Henley we are going to see a big increase in interest in the performing arts on the big screen. The limiting factor is likely to be the attitude of the theatres and the loss of live audiences. At the moment the choice is not great but price will be a limiting factor and people will become more selective. [385]

> I think it's a very practical clever way to get more people to appreciate the arts within a reasonable budget. Going to the Opera House in Covent Garden or New York is something not accessible to most otherwise. The adventure was new to me and totally riveting. Please do more. [271]

> Wonderful life-enhancing experience. In these very doom-laden times (dire political situation nationally and internationally etc) and with toxic/mediocre television programming (reality shows, Jeremy Kyle etc), it was magical to be enjoying beautiful music in such an immediate close-up way, and to know that others in 40 countries were also enjoying it at the same time. [166]

The common feature in such responses is the simple celebration of quality. But to that is added, to varying degrees, the notion that these events may be doing other important work. They are taking theatre, opera and other such cultural forms out of an elite enclosure. They are reaching global audiences, making such works accessible to a wider range of people, perhaps adding a democratic, even civilising, dimension to them. To think about this strand, one has to return to the work of Pierre Bourdieu.

Bourdieu developed an elaborate theorisation of the interconnections between economic, cultural and symbolic forms of capital, and argued that it was in and through both choices of cultural forms and ways of participating in them that people produced themselves as members of their society. In his key book *Distinction* (1979), which was based on an extensive survey in 1960s France, he made a broad distinction between high cultures of choice (in which art galleries, classical music and the like bulked large, and which required a knowing gaze) and low cultures of necessity (popular music and dance, to be immediately and sensuously enjoyed, exemplified these). Each of these has its own tradition, of course, its historically developed 'field' of production and circulation. High-culture fields will tend to include reviewers, experts, connoisseurs, educators, academics. Low-culture fields will more likely bring together commercial producers selling excitement to fans. Critical to Bourdieu's conception was that these different modes were hierarchically organised, carrying value and prestige at their height, but dismissed and even

DOI: 10.1057/9781137288691

reviled at the bottom. People live their choices and positions within such a hierarchy, through internalising and naturalising culturally learnt preferences ('habitus') and even through learnt bodily responses ('hexis').

The work in which these ideas become most concrete, and which is perhaps most applicable to livecasts, is his study on photography (Bourdieu, 1996). Bourdieu explored and compared the ways in which three Paris photographic clubs made judgements about what makes a good photograph. An art club placed its emphasis on the formal properties of a picture (lighting, focus, composition etc.) and paid little attention to its subject-matter. By sharp contrast, a club of industrial workers at the Renault works chose photographs which captured treasured moments and stories from their lives – in significant senses photographs that they could show and share. The third club, sponsored by an equipment manufacturer, embodied what they called a 'middle-brow taste'. Its members sought to produce 'artistic' works, but lacked the cultural capital to match the art club. They tended instead towards conventionalised and often sentimental subjects. It is the implications of that third position, with its uneasy balancing act, which I return to later.

Bourdieu's work has spawned a huge industry of debate and commentary. Many scholars have questioned whether Bourdieu's findings apply outside the narrow context of 1960s France (and studies in other countries have suggested otherwise; see, for instance, Bennett et al., 1999, on Australia, and Bennett and Savage, 2010, on the UK). I mentioned earlier the work of Peterson and Kern on the replacement of 'univores' by 'omnivores'. In France, a next generation of scholars has modified Bourdieu's grand scheme, retaining his hierarchical awareness, but for instance emphasising its operation within specific genres and fields (see, for instance, Glévarec, 2005; Maigret, 2012). But despite these and other debates his work has generated, I believe it is still possible to say that while many critics have challenged his particular concepts and conclusions, his *questions* about the hierarchical nature of culture, and the relations of this hierarchy to power and wealth, have remained. Others indeed have added to them. Lawrence Levine's (1990) study of the seizure of Shakespeare as 'high culture' in nineteenth-century America, Richard Butsch's (2000) work on the transformation of theatre and cinema audiences across two centuries in the same country and John Storey's (2010) work on the bourgeois capture of opera in mid-nineteenth-century Manchester have all fleshed out such processes. And it is noticeable that critics of Bourdieu tend to go to statistical evidence, for evidence *that*

DOI: 10.1057/9781137288691

people are participating, while his supporters attend more qualitatively to evidence on *how* people participate.

One aspect of Bourdieu's work has received less attention, but is important to the topic of livecasts. The aspect I am concerned with is Bourdieu's approach to the state. While he is clearly intensely aware of the role of the state in relation to culture (he carried out numerous studies on the French education system), his overarching account emphasises the *separating* of classes, the role of education in preparing people for their class-station in life and the marking off of cultural forms. This leaves little space for what appears to be going on with livecasts. For in the UK at least there is a clear tendency for the research on and promotion of livecasts to be presented as part of a *tendency to wish to spread high (good) culture to the less fortunate*. This is culture with a social purpose, promising moral uplift. Under the influence of New Labour, which sought to redefine poverty, unemployment and disadvantage as 'social exclusion', there came initiatives to encourage cultural participation (see, for instance, Department of Culture, Media and Sport, 2008). This required of museums, for instance, that they proved they were reaching out to people who would not normally visit. Arts venues seeking funding from bodies such as the Arts Council had to demonstrate that they were seeking new audiences. A series of researches, reports and initiatives across the 1990s promulgated these ideas. At the same time, various media, but especially television, produced a series of programmes premised on the idea of showing the masses the joys of the arts. Among others, the film *Billy Elliot* (Stephen Daldry, 2000) followed the son of a miner who just wanted to be a ballet dancer, and the cultural conflicts this set in motion. BBC2's *The Choir* across three series took untrained singers and trained them under a professional choir-master. Channel 4's *Operatunity* adapted the reality TV format to go searching for opera stars in the general population. These and others seemed to live out the Blairite ideals of 'social inclusion', of showing ordinary people how rich their cultural lives could be, what Sarah Martindale (2011) has usefully called 'art as social service'.

Such social democratic interventions were inevitably lived out differently in the USA, where the idea of government interventions in culture is almost anathema (think of the almost continuous round of criticisms of the National Endowment for the Arts whenever its funding looks even minimally political). Even here, though, there have been pressures for the arts to prove their *usefulness*. I referred earlier to the WolfBrown Report which sought to develop measures for the 'intrinsic value of the arts' (Brown and Novak, 2007). But what was driving that Report and

DOI: 10.1057/9781137288691

others like it[1] perhaps comes most clearly into view in an earlier Report, *Reggae to Rachmaninoff* (Walker and Scott-Melnyk, 2002). This Report appears assiduously apolitical. Deliberately adopting a broad definition of cultural participation, it argues that more people are in fact taking part in some kind of cultural activity than commonly supposed – and it doesn't matter whether this is church choirs, art galleries, amateur theatre or jazz. But the authors then identify a *kind* of participant who is more 'civic-minded' than the rest. Here is their icon, their model citizen who will save America from a feared loss of community cohesion – a loss which had become a topic of increasing political debate from the mid-1990s, and which was crystallised in Robert Putnam's highly controversial *Bowling Alone* (2000). Putnam's claim was to show that there had been a steady decline in civic participation in American communities. The arts were being given the job of remedying some of this. Walker and Scott-Melnyk identify the potential new heroes: 'These activists represent a bridge between the world of arts and culture and community-building efforts, and they are a potential resource for community building' (2002: 24). The list of arts with such capacities turns out to be depressingly restricted, after their wide opening definition: 'music, dance, theater, and visual arts' (2002: 59).

Livecasting, then, emerged into a charged context in which 'the arts' were increasingly being checked for their measurable worth and social contribution. It is no surprise, in this context, that among the headlines drawn from NESTA's research with NT Live was that emphasis on the combined facts that the National Theatre's cinema audiences had overall lower incomes, but reported higher levels of both enthusiasm and involvement.

The wider value of livecasts

What should we say, in light of these issues, about the ways in which audiences are perceiving the wider benefits of livecasts? In fact, the first thing to be said is how *unusual* those responses quoted at the start of this chapter were. More commonly, if my respondents wanted to say something about other audiences, they were complaining about inappropriate behaviour:

> Audiences sometimes act like cinema is telly in their own sitting rooms: chatting eating etc. [401]

DOI: 10.1057/9781137288691

> Audience behaviour: Last night the audience were not only permitted to take drinks but actual bottles of wine into the auditorium – there was even a sales promotion at the bar encouraging this. I had to move seats last night and was lucky to find two seats spare. Had that not happened I would have left the performance and believe me I would not be returning. Nobody is questioning the right of the cinema to maximise profit which can subsidise great cinema to considerably sparse audiences but taking a bottle in is too much and I cannot tolerate that. [4]

> The audience in the cinema had lots of popcorn etc which hasn't yet hit the theatre. Also chattering etc. I find both of these off-putting and on the whole theatre audiences don't eat or talk and I prefer this. [136]

Just occasionally, they were regretting how narrow the range of people who attended was ('I wish the audiences were more mixed – how can the cinema attract some younger people? [493]). But if there is a recurrent thread in the way my respondents talked about the wider reach, it is almost entirely restricted to a wish for international companies to come to them. The best of the world ought to be available. This feeling underpins a good number of the responses to my final question: whether there is a 'dream event' that they would love to see. The following are typical:

> The Met engages the world's top singers none of whom sing in Aberdeen and only a few of whom I can ever hope to see at the Edinburgh International Festival or in London – and occasionally in New York. We heard outstanding singing in Tosca. [228]

> Doesn't match the real thing but is good enough to have a good night out especially with a Cambridge audience of opera buffs. Seeing live opera with leading and up and coming international singers without having to travel around the world and pay high prices is a great opportunity. [411]

This is a case of 'the best should come to us'. If there is an identifiable tenor to the few responses which hint at a possible educative role for livecasts, it strikes me that it is one of mild self-mockery, with almost no substantive content, as here:

> The fact that famous operas can be put to the reach of many who may not be able to afford going to the Opera House or even ENO in London is a way of educating the masses! MANY people may have heard of some works but it is out of their pockets. It is convenient to go to the local cinema and on a large screen one is totally immersed with the characters. [546]

New Labour rhetorics on things of this kind have gone into near-terminal decline. In fact, currently, it would not be exaggerating to say

DOI: 10.1057/9781137288691

that the term 'culture' has taken on a decidedly grubby tone, typified by the following uses in recent UK press talk: box-ticking culture, culture of greed and self-interest, drug culture, gang culture, machismo culture, bonus culture, culture of bullying, anti-business culture, compensation culture, culture of outrage, culture of illegal payments, 'something for nothing' culture, health and safety culture, culture of institutional racism, culture of bullying, yob culture, celebrity-driven culture, culture of 'abortions on demand', 'bung' culture and kids who have no culture.[2] Overwhelmingly, talk of 'culture' has moved out of the positive realm to constitute an attack on excuses, or constraints, or inability. It is hard, in this context, to make believable claims for the benefits of culture. Partly, then, my suspicion is that people talking in this way simply want to be able to talk positively about culture. They are refusing to be embarrassed about their pleasures, and the importance which they attach to them. They would quite like to share them – although only on condition that other audiences behave themselves.

Beyond this, my argument would be that we should stay away from exaggerated claims about any wider benefits or implications of livecasting. Strident claims about changes in the overall scale and hierarchy of culture and the arts are part of the running rhetoric of contemporary society. Yet for all that, I think there are signs of unease around the emergence of livecasting. Yes, it is a relatively cheap way for people to get to see things otherwise denied to them. It allows local passions for opera in particular to be lived. In the other direction, it upsets those for whom such experiences can only be had 'pure', at source. The signs are not yet clear. But there is a clear historical tradition of unease at the middle-brow – a sense that culture improperly used demeans itself – which may be recurring here. And people responding with self-irony about 'the masses' could usefully be understood as responding in kind.

I am not alone in wondering about these things. I close this chapter with another person's amused thoughts on the implications of this. The unorthodox cellist Jon Silpayamanant, who regularly blogs his thoughts on musical issues, wrote in 2011 about seeing fliers at his local cinema for the Met's livecasts. Intriguing, he thought, and headlined his remarks 'The Death of the Cinematic Industry': 'For all the folks who continue to maintain the popularity of pop culture – in conjunction with the supposed decline of high culture (Classical Music) – it's a bit ironic that movie theaters are now showing live casts of, well, classical music.' But an unease runs through Silpayamanant's comments, partly about the

DOI: 10.1057/9781137288691

loss of work opportunities that might follow, but partly also about the *appropriateness* of listening to an orchestra in the wrong place. There is a lurking sense of uncertainty, of the unknown, in discussions of this kind.

This is really the tip of an iceberg of ideas and debates. Important work on ideas of cultural hierarchy, and on Bourdieu's work on this subject, is going on at this time, and I can only hope that this book will make some contribution.

Notes

1   See also, for instance, Ostrower (2005), which opens with these words: 'Those who wish to understand or expand cultural participation need to pay greater attention to its diversity.'
2   All these were found by searching in the UK press over just one month in 2011, in the Nexis press database.

DOI: 10.1057/9781137288691

7
The Next Research Tasks?

Abstract: *To conclude, this chapter poses a series of further research questions, and explains their importance to the full understanding of livecasting. It looks across to the political economy of culture; to issues of intellectual property and rights management (and other associated legal issues); to debates about the future of cinema as, potentially, a site of multiple arts provision; to the processes whereby the emergent aesthetics of these events might sediment and standardise – and in consequence to the future attitudes towards them of academics (for many of whom issues around 'liveness' carry heavy theoretical and even political loads); and to the potentials for future research into audiences for these kinds of events, and how the idea of the 'cinema audience' might be altered as a result.*

Barker, Martin. *Live To Your Local Cinema: The Remarkable Rise of Livecasting*. Basingstoke: Palgrave Macmillan, 2013. DOI: 10.1057/9781137288691.

In this book I hope I have opened up for critical thought and investigation many of the issues raised by the emergence of Alternative Content – or livecasting, as I have riskily chosen to call it – in cinemas. In this closing chapter I want to point to some major questions which are raised by my account, but which I have not had the chance – and may lack the skills – to research.

Some of the questions posed by this book essentially involve extensions and deepenings of its evidence. Inevitably, I am able to say more about the UK and other Anglophone countries than about the rest of the world. Simply extending coverage to a wider range of countries will surely change some parts of my portrait. Digital equipment has penetrated various countries by different routes (therefore arriving first at, and privileging, different sorts of cinema) and to different degrees (therefore altering the extent to which livecasting affects the overall ecology of cinemas' income). These are important issues in their own right. A separate set of questions will be raised by the different status that art-forms have in various national cultures. Opera is much more a cross-class phenomenon in a country such as Italy, for instance, than it is in Britain; likewise ballet in Russia (and of course if you cross-relate that with the issue of whether livecasting – other than of the Bolshoi Ballet itself – has penetrated the former Soviet bloc countries to any degree, the picture will get even more complicated).

But it is not really these extensions and deepenings that concern me here. Instead, I want to sketch some topics that are at present beyond me, in the hope that other researchers will find an impulse to address them.

1   The political economy of livecasts

Political economy, as I understand it, is the study of the systems through which goods (in this case cultural goods) are produced, marketed and used. How do different systems and their attendant institutions work, and to whose benefit? And what effect do the operations of such systems have on the *kinds* of goods that are produced? Within political economy generally, there is a widespread recognition that cultural industries work in some distinctive ways. The most convincing explanation that I know for this is a combination of two approaches. The first has been well stated by Nick Garnham, who argued some years ago (with his eye on Hollywood) that cultural production is driven by the need to handle the

DOI: 10.1057/9781137288691

challenge that each new output has to be in some senses a prototype. Old films may of course be occasionally re-released, but every studio has to keep making and releasing new films, whose success is largely unpredictable. This, Garnham argues, puts a premium on all kinds of procedures for managing and controlling distribution: 'It is cultural distribution, not cultural production, that is the key locus of power and profit' (1990: 161–2). The second approach, pretty much the flipside of the first, is the idea that cultural goods are 'experience goods' – that is, things which we cannot be sure we will enjoy until we have consumed them (see Nelson, 1970, for one of the early statements of this). Audiences therefore seek knowledge and reassurance in advance of purchase. There is a cascade of possibilities connecting these two elements: publicity promises, reputation and known elements (genres, sequels, actors, authors, brands etc.), reviews, gossip, word-of-mouth recommendations. All these and many more bring a degree of predictability into an uncertain sphere. They are all relevant to a new business like this one. So, my first proposed questions are these: *[1] How are producers and distributors learning to manage the risks in this branch of cultural production? How is competition between major players organised, and what spaces are there for fringe producers? [2] How is livecasting affecting the broader ecology of cinema, and the existing relationships between film producers and cinema owners? How in particular do the major studios respond to its rise?*

Unsurprisingly, the large companies involved in this emergent business are quite coy about its economics. But it is clear that a lot of thinking and research has gone into creating business models for its development. If it is clear that the New York Met entered pell-mell because of the emergent structural hole in their funding sources, it is harder to determine how far its success has resolved its crisis, in the medium and long term. People have commented cynically on the Met's protectionist strategy (trying to corner the market for livecast opera by insisting that cinemas receiving their broadcasts take no competing materials during the season). That clearly is part of one business model.

An important question, then, is: how have the various companies formed and tested their picture of the market, and what has been taken into account? We can begin to form a picture of some of the considerations from the questions asked in the commercially oriented research. They needed to ask what kinds of broadcast would be likely to attract audiences, what prices audiences would be willing to pay, whether there

DOI: 10.1057/9781137288691

was an interest in buying recordings of performances they had seen, and what factors in performances added to or subtracted from their pleasure and interest. But other factors are surely likely to be in play. How will this new business need to be promoted, and how might such promotion affect the 'brands' of different companies? What risks are there of offending their older, core audience? What kinds of stars might best 'lead' their offerings?

This, then, is my next group of questions: *[3] How have the various companies formed, elaborated and tested business models for the future of this kind of cultural provision? What kinds of audience research have fed into these? How are these models informing their decisions and plans (including for kinds of content)?*

A different sort of political-economic question is posed by the distribution of the spoils. People buying tickets to livecast events generally are aware of two things: they are paying *above* film prices, but *well below* prices at the source-event. And the cinemas are often full, if not sold out. This suggests a large pot of additional money flowing through the systems. But it is not yet clear where the bulk of the benefit is falling. The carve-up of earnings between producers, distributors, satellite handlers and exhibitors is one such unknown. Typically, NT Live's contracts require a split as follows: NT Live 45 per cent, Picturehouse (for all aspects of distribution) 10 per cent, cinemas 45 per cent. (For films, let it be noted, the split commonly leaves 65–70 per cent to cinemas, depending on proximity to initial release.) Clearly there are new costs involved: the adaptation and equipping of theatres to enable effective recording (although some of these costs will be non-recurring), hiring specialist staff to design and conduct the recordings, satellite transmission (and associated) costs and different kinds of publicity. Even so, we can be sure, just from the overall number of tickets sold, that substantial additional income is being generated. The question is: who is benefiting? Anecdotal evidence from talking with cinema managers suggests to me that for venues the income gain can be quite marginal. Cinemas will pay for the event itself and for transmission rights, and often ticket prices are partly set for them. In addition, the length of performances – especially when intervals are counted in – can mean they supplant two film screenings. Income received must therefore cover at least what could have been earned from two film events. A full house is clearly going to be profitable. But it may well be that less than a sell-out is more risky than a film, with its lower fixed costs.

Accordingly, my next follow-up question is: *[4] How is income distributed along the chain, from production companies, through distributors, digital enablers, to venues? Where are the risks mainly borne, and what is the prevailing balance of forces and influences allowing some to benefit more than others?*

I am certain that readers with a background in economics or business studies will be able to put these questions better than I have, or come up with others.

2 Rights management and power-plays

Inevitably, the rise of Alternative Content (and here it does seem appropriate to use the industry's term) has given rise to a run of new contractual and legal issues – some predictable, others not. Intellectual property rights have been said to be the fastest growth area in law over the past few decades. And certainly issues from this domain – most notably the problems of residuals (who can claim earnings from subsequent screenings) – are among the issues which have impeded subsequent DVD releases of livecasts.

But this is by no means the only issue. There can be specific extra fees, for instance for what is known as Grand Rights (a legal term relating to ownership of copyright in original materials). There can also be a minimum fee, payable regardless of audience size. This last is probably not a concern with popular events but can be a real threat to cinemas' margins when they think of taking one-off, experimental or unproven materials. (*Caligula*, a ballet from Opéra National de Paris, did spectacularly badly across the UK in 2011; this, along with experiences of poor transmission, led to non-renewal of contracts.)

Producing companies also put requirements on ticket prices. NT Live currently (2012) requires that cinemas do not charge more than £15 per seat in the UK, as part of compliance with its outreach strategy – an important condition, among other things, of its state funding. The New York Met on the other hand sets a *minimum* price, taking 50 per cent of the house (and cinemas have to pay separately about $250 for digital transmission). But in the Met's contract are clauses of far greater import. In a move oddly reminiscent of the kinds of contract between producers and cinemas in the 1930s, which were outlawed by the 1948 Paramount Act, cinemas receiving the Met's season (and they cannot just pick individual livecasts) may not take any other livecast opera for that period plus 30 days. (In 2011 the Met tried to make this 120 days, but encountered serious protests.) Glyndebourne, a relative late-comer, took a similar

DOI: 10.1057/9781137288691

course. Offering a season of three live and three recorded broadcasts, they refused to allow cinemas to opt only for the former, although experience has shown that even a 24-hour delay reduces audience interest substantially. (Glyndebourne did not, mind, impose a minimum fee.)

All these illustrations indicate that, as so often, legal and contractual issues are also the sites of power-plays. And this clearly invites more systematic enquiry by legal specialists. Tentatively thinking how the questions might be posed, I would wonder: *[5] How have contractual relations evolved during the early history of Alternative Content? What general and specific laws have been seen to apply to the arrangements? What exemplary cases and precedents will emerge, perhaps differently by country, to regulate relations between the various players?*

A different set of questions arises from the distinctive context posed by European law. A fundamental principle underpinning the European Union is the promotion of borderless free trade – but an exception is allowed where actions are taken in the interest of the protection of 'national culture'. This get-out clause has been extensively used by various countries to regulate ownership of the media, for instance. It led to a series of verbal manoeuvres when the British Government sought to justify its provision of tax breaks for British film-makers. The possible implications of this are many, not least when bodies funded by the Arts Council (easily defensible on cultural grounds) move out of their theatres into more overtly 'commercial' sectors. So: *[6] How will regional laws and regulations impact on the evolution of Alternative Content as a business?*

3   Future architectures

How secure the future business of Alternative Content is cannot be known with certainty. And that is an issue both for those involved in it and for people like myself who are studying it. One salient factor is, simply, the confidence that major players feel in its growth and importance to the business of cinema (not film). And one way in which this can assayed over the next few years is in the designing and planning of new cinemas.

It is well known to historians of cinema that the design, location and appeal of cinemas have gone through definite waves (for two good general histories of cinema architecture, see van Uffelen, 2009, and Gray, 2010). From converted store-front spaces to the first specialist houses;

DOI: 10.1057/9781137288691

from picture palaces to modernist boxes; and then, after the recovery from the massive post-World War II decline in attendance, the rise of the mall-sited multiplexes, alongside a smattering of smaller, specialist art-house cinemas (sometimes in arts complexes, sometimes in genteel conversions). Building has proceeded in cycles and waves, driven by general economic conditions of course, but also by developers' perceptions of audience trends and confidence in the industry's near future. The wave of multiplex building, located especially in out-of-town shopping centres, developed in the 1980s but has been in decline for the past decade. Their typically anonymous, shell-like, sharply-lit spaces with large foyers lacking seating areas and emphasising additional sales, with blank corridors into identical screens, all resonating with the styles and ambience of the malls: these packages placed films as experiences to be had between buying trainers and having a Big Mac. And the association between multiplexes, with their massive sound-systems, and the big loud blockbuster is no accident. While not a universal model, the multiplex has certainly been the dominant *idea* of a contemporary cinema.

The question thus arises: following the recent slowdown in cinema building, to what extent will the major developers feel that the potential for future business has to take into account the audiences and their expectations for livecasting? They are older, and more middle-class. They want a night out, and take the whole experience quite seriously. They are likely to want pleasant circulation spaces, programmes, seats, good toilets, a sense of a building's identity. They assuredly dislike the intrusion of loud pop music. The point of comparison therefore will not be the mall, but theatres maybe, with posters, photographs of players, a sense of cultural history. This is not the same as the recent announcement of plans by Cineworld of their search for good locations for a next generation of 'luxury cinemas', intended to provide gourmet screen experiences – of a kind that roused Ryan Gilbey (2012) to a froth of indignation (he scorned the provision of 'triple-cushioned, sofa-size seats', 'fancy-pants auditoria' and 'truffle-oil drizzled' accompaniments – all of which speak of the equivalent of airlines' 'priority boarding' regimes). No, this would be cinema design for a different mode of cultural use. An interesting research task, then, will be to track over the next 10 years the thoughts, planning and decisions in different areas and countries: *[7] Do cinema developers presume Alternative Content to be a brief comet, best left to specialist providers? Or could this become core business, to be nurtured with newly conceived cinema designs and locations?*

DOI: 10.1057/9781137288691

4   Emergent aesthetics

My research into livecasts has, hopefully, caught a new bird just leaving its nest. Plumage and song are not yet fully developed; flight patterns are still being learnt. But already, perhaps, some of the adult characteristics can be seen. And it is certain that those who contribute professionally to the business are moving between safe formula and cautious experimentation.

There is clear evidence that in these initial stages the outside broadcast is providing one model for designing the capture of livecast performances. The models here are big sports events, pop concerts and media spectacles. But some aspects of these are simply very different. The management of replay in sports events, the use of multiple screens in large concerts, zippy camera movements and visible mikes and cameras are simply not appropriate. And there is the added requirement for the whole mediation process to be as unobtrusive as possible, both to the theatre audience and to the cinema recipients. In short, producers are having to turn a set of constraints into a new aesthetic. This raises a tangle of questions. What training regimes will emerge for camera operators, lighting designers, sound recordists and live editors? Will theatre directors try out new modes of use of the stage and relations with audiences? How soon will training companies incorporate consideration of this mode of address into their practices? In short: *[8] How will the Alternative Content business professionalise itself?*

In Chapter 2, I gave a very preliminary analysis of some of the emergent aesthetics of livecasts. But I placed a self-imposed limit on what I discussed there. What I didn't discuss, and what remain very much to be investigated, are the ways in which these emergent aesthetics affect livecast works' designers and performers. One indication of the challenges here was given in a rather sharp article in the *New York Times* (2012), in which Zachary Woolfe explored what he identified as some 'subtle shifts' he had identified in the New York Met's recent productions. He listed a growing emphasis on small gestures and facial movements, more suited to camera than large theatre; more restrained voices, where good mike capture can ensure a rich expressiveness is experienced; the greater impact of physical actions (he gives the example of a slap, which hardly registered with the theatre audience, but startled some cinema viewers). Writing personally, he declared: 'When I saw Natalie Dessay at the Met in "Lucia di Lammermoor" in February 2011, her radically introverted

DOI: 10.1057/9781137288691

conception of the role seemed simply dull and detached; later in HD it was haunting.' To the extent that livecasts become economically essential to the Met, that may mean their privileging the cinema audience's experience over the house audience's. We need to ask: *[9] In what ways and through what mechanisms do producers and performers learn to adjust their work to their understanding of the new medium?*

One question which pretty evidently teases me concerns attitudes towards 'liveness'. When I began researching livecasting in 2009, I became aware of suspicion bordering on hostility among a number of colleagues in the theatre and performance world. Livecasts were a threat to their sense of self, their way of being performance professionals. For all the debates within theatre and performance studies around Auslander's book – whose limits anyway are pretty much the incorporation of elements of mediation *within* a performance – liveness is a *commitment* for many practitioners. It has for them a guaranteed superiority over any more distanced forms. (For a recent example of the fears this engenders, see Nick Moran's revealingly entitled 2010 essay 'Resisting the Lure of the Screen'.) As I began work on this book, I was hearing of papers on the topic at theatre and performance conferences. It will be fascinating to watch the evolution of debates about the 'liveness' of livecasts – not least because this will play a part in the speed at which theatre educators take up the topic in curricula. So: *[10] How will debates on the relevance and challenges of Alternative Content, particularly in relation to their challenges to conceptualisations of 'liveness', play out within proximal academic fields?*

5   The audience

My interest in this whole phenomenon began from the confluence of my personal attendance at NT Live's *Phèdre* and questions that arose from my intellectual position as an audience researcher. The research which I did in association with Picturehouse Cinemas and my exploration of commercial researches in this area all flowed from this. But I was researching as the egg was hatching, and that surely makes a difference. Many of my respondents were talking about attending their very first livecast. I was, then, in something like the same position as researchers who went to observe the arrival of television in particular communities. But the problem of those early TV researchers was precisely that they didn't take much account of

DOI: 10.1057/9781137288691

the sheer fact of *novelty*. New technologies, new modes of culture, take time to settle. Early adopters, indeed, are not a good guide to subsequent status. So, how long will it remain true that the predominant audience is over 65? How soon will the currently grumpy participants – those with the strongest purist tendencies over 'liveness' – give up and leave the fray? The best model I could find for thinking about the kinds of 'liveness' that livecasts offer is pub football audiences, for all their (class, locality, allegiance) differences. Nonetheless, it does raise a question about how far livecasts' cinema audiences might find ways to constitute themselves *as communities*, with regular attendance, senses of membership and shared rituals.

Audience research remains the orphan child of academic work in the theatre and performance, music and comedy fields, and even (despite somewhat greater growth) in the film and television arenas. And academic audience research which speaks with practitioners is even rarer. The question I want to pose here therefore consciously comes out of a conversation I recently had with a cinema manager about his sense of livecasts' audiences. Asked what he thought made livecasts most likely to be successful, after a pause he offered one word: 'familiarity'. As we talked about the meanings of this word, a number of possibilities came into view: known plays, operas and so on, recognisable names (stars) or brands (companies), and 'intimate' surroundings (he noted his deliberate practice of giving people numbered seats – something they would recognise from theatres, but which is very rare in cinemas). All of which point towards one large, to me fascinating, question: *[11] In what ways do livecast audiences hope and try to recreate cinema spaces as theatrical spaces? How are they evolving theatre-like 'manners', and how are these experienced and learnt by newcomers and interlopers?*

6   New developments in adaptation studies

One reader for the proposal for this book pointed to a significant gap in its coverage. Nothing that I wrote linked the study of livecasts with the big changes that have taken place in the past two decades in adaptation studies. I acknowledge the truth of this, but with the excuse that in the relatively constricted space of this Palgrave Pivot, it is simply not possible to do everything. And, to be honest, although in a general way I know the shape of the developments, it is not my home territory. All I can do is to point to some potential questions.

DOI: 10.1057/9781137288691

For a long time, adaptation studies was dominated by two concerns: medium theory (that is, an interest in the special characteristics that distinguish the novel, say, from the film) and 'faithfulness' (that is, a consideration of how much is lost when, say, a novel is translated to film – and this was and remains one of the most potent relationships). After a long gestation period, a point of change was perhaps reached in 2004, with the publication of two major books by Robert Stam and Alessandra Raengo. Alongside these sprang up an Association of Adaptation Studies and two journals, *Adaptation* and *Journal of Adaptation in Film and Performance*, all devoted to studying much more broadly the textual, contextual, paratextual, historical, institutional and reception aspects of adaptation (this list is compiled from the two journals' self-descriptions). A third journal, *Literature and Film*, reoriented itself under a new editor in the same period. Perhaps as important as the broadening was the shift away from making normative judgements ('this version is superior to that version'). Clearly the potentials for studying livecasts within this broadened frame are great – but with a need to complicate one of those dimensions. 'Reception' would need to include the impact of *mode of delivery*. In many ways, livecasts try to deny that they are adaptations – it is only that we get to see and hear performances by a different means. We have seen that for some audiences that makes a crucial difference. For others, it might be more akin to the difference between reading a physical book and reading on a Kindle (unless of course you want to say that that *does* make a significant difference). Perhaps one way to frame this as a question will be simply to ask: *[12] When, and to whom, does a livecast become an 'adaptation'?*

7   Control and censorship

A minor, but still fascinating, strand of future enquiry will be to consider the ways in which livecasts come to be placed for censorship purposes. Theatre censorship in the UK was abolished in 1967. Cinema censorship partially transmogrified into classification with the renaming of the British Board of Film Censors in 1984. Film classification is now subject to a whole range of legal constraints, as Julian Petley (2011) has recently summarised, whereas theatre is, at worst, subject to possible *post facto* prosecutions for obscenity (as happened, notoriously, with Mary Whitehouse's attempted prosecution of *The Romans in Britain* in

DOI: 10.1057/9781137288691

1980). The BBFC has tried to keep a careful distance from what it has called 'as-live' screenings, ostensibly on the grounds that it was just not feasible to classify livecasts as they went out. It also allowed a seven-day period of grace for subsequent screenings, to enable delayed transmissions, and repeats. One livecast at least, though, stepped beyond this. Danny Boyle's *Frankenstein* proved sufficiently popular to produce later repeat screenings, was submitted to the BBFC and came back with a '15' certificate. Thus, a theatrical event which, so theatre scholars will insist, is more powerful when live than it could ever be when mediated has no restrictions at its source, but an age-limitation at the cinema.[1]

Such oddities and inconsistencies are now standard as different kinds of 'convergence' mean that cultural materials become available through multiple channels. The future of this with respect to 'high culture', which has often more fiercely defended its right to take risks and to challenge audiences, is worth watching. The history of legal controls over cinema is one of the adaptation of licensing regulations (for fire and safety purposes) over which have been laid more and more layers of moral paintwork, until – like a Rachel Whiteread house – the shell is all that remains. But that has always been premised on untested notions that watching films carries a danger of possible 'harm' that does not attend less 'popular' art-forms. So, finally: *[13] How do law and practice develop and proceed on the 'acceptable limits' of livecasts, what self-denying decisions are made by producers, and what stress-points emerge as we move into the next, more settled – but therefore perhaps more experimental – phase of this development?*

8   The naming of parts

Finally, I remain fascinated by what this whole phenomenon will come to be called – and of course by what will be seen to be implied by that name once it has sedimented. 'Alternative Content' is less a name, more a pointer. It is hard to attach *any* adjectives to such a hollow expression. How can someone be a 'fan', or 'connoisseur', or 'addict', or 'buff' of something so bland and empty? Settling a name for 'livecasts' will be part of settling their status, as a set of discourses and status-markers assemble around them.

On 7 September 2012, 70 people from six countries gathered in London to launch a new trade association for the Alternative Content industry. Distributors, exhibitors and, unusually, content providers began to share

DOI: 10.1057/9781137288691

ideas on how to build public recognition of this whole area of cinema provision. This is an important development, and it will be fascinating to track its course over the next few years. But what is immediately interesting is the organisation's name: the Event Cinema Association. Clearly people inside the industry are as aware as I have been of the need for a workable public name – something by which these events can be known and talked about without quotation marks. Will this name, 'Event Cinema', spread and stick, or will it stay only a trade name? To answer that right now would be pure guesswork. But it is striking that among the tasks that the Association took on itself was to educate journalists in these new developments. And journalists sometimes work as linguistic taste-makers.

Note

1   The arbitrariness involved here is emphasised by the fact that in its theatrical version the Monster at birth was completely naked – whereas for the livecast filming he was given a breech-cloth. Thus, the age-restricted version ended up being more 'protective' than the unrestricted!

DOI: 10.1057/9781137288691

References

Abel, Sam (1996) *Opera in the Flesh: Sexuality in Performance*, Boulder, CO: Westview Press.

Altman, Rick (1999) *Film/Genre*, London: BFI.

Anderson, Louise (2010) 'Else-when and Else-where: The Formation of Newsreel Memory as a Distinctive Type of Popular Cultural Memory', PhD Thesis, University of Newcastle.

Arts Council (2008) 'Arts Audiences: Insight'. Found at: http://www.artscouncil.org.uk/publication_archive/arts-audiences-insight/.

Auslander, Philip (1999) *Liveness*, London: Routledge.

Baker, Camille C. (2011) 'MINDtouch – Embodied Ephemeral Transference: Mobile Media Performance Research', *International Journal of Performance Arts and Digital Media*, 7:1, 97–116.

Bakhshi, Hasan and David Throsby (2009) 'Innovation in Arts and Cultural Organisations', NESTA Interim Research Report 1, December. Found at: http://www.nesta.org.uk/library/documents/Innovation-in-arts-and-cultural-interim.pdf.

Balme, Christopher B. (2008a) *The Cambridge Introduction to Theatre Studies*, Cambridge: Cambridge University Press.

Balme, Christopher (2008b) 'Surrogate Stages: Theatre, Performance and the Challenge of New Media', *Performance Research*, 13:2, 80–91.

Barker, Martin (2003) '*Crash*, Theatre Audiences, and the Idea of "Liveness"', *Studies in Theatre and Performance*, 23:1, 21–39.

DOI: 10.1057/9781137288691

Barker, Martin (2012) 'Crossing Out the Audience', in Ian Christie (ed.), *Audiences*, Amsterdam: Amsterdam University Press.

Barr, Charles (1996) ' "They Think It's All Over": The Dramatic Legacy of Live Television', in John Hill and Martin McLoone (eds), *Big Picture, Small Screen: The Relations between Film and Television*, Luton: John Libbey Media, pp. 47–75.

Belsey, Catherine (1983) 'Shakespeare and Film: A Question of Perspective', *Literature/Film Quarterly*, 11:3, 152–8.

Bennett, Lucy (2011) 'Listening through Social Media: Online Fan Engagement with the Live Music Experience'. Paper presented at *Transforming Audiences 3*: 'Online & Mobile Media, Everyday Creativity and DIY Culture', University of Westminster, London, 1–2 September.

Bennett, Tony and Mike Savage (2010) *Culture, Class, Distinction*, London: Routledge.

Bennett, Tony, Michael Emmison and John Frow (1999) *Accounting for Tastes: Australian Everyday Cultures*, Cambridge: Cambridge University Press.

Biron, Dean (2009) 'Betwixt and Between: Musical Taste Patterns and Audience Mobility', *Participations: Online Journal of Audience and Reception Studies*, 6:2. Found at: http://www.participations.org/Volume%206/Issue%202/biron.htm.

Bode, Lisa (2010) 'No Longer Themselves: Framing Digitally Enabled Posthumous "Performance" ', *Cinema Journal*, 49:4, 46–70.

Bourdieu, Pierre (1979) *La Distinction: Critique sociale du jugement*, Paris: Editions de Minuit.

Bourdieu, Pierre (1996) *Photography: A Middle-Brow Art*, Cambridge: Polity.

Brown, Alan S. and Jennifer L. Novak (2007) *Assessing the Intrinsic Value of a Live Performance*, San Francisco: WolfBrown.

Brown, Kevin (2010) 'Liveness Anxiety: Karaoke and the Performance of Class', *Popular Entertainment Studies*, 1:2, 61–77.

Butsch, Richard (2000) *The Making of American Audiences: From Stage to Television, 1750–1990*, Cambridge: Cambridge University Press.

Canadian Corporate Newswire (2001) 'Boeing to Deliver "Jekyll & Hyde" by Satellite for Broadway Television Network', 27 April.

Citron, Marcia J. (2000) *Opera on Screen*, New Haven, CT: Yale University Press.

Crawford, Garry (2008) 'Consuming Sport, Consuming Beer: Sport Fans, Scene and Everyday Life', in Lawrence A. Wenner and Steven

DOI: 10.1057/9781137288691

J. Jackson (eds), *Sport, Beer, and Gender: Promotional Culture &
Contemporary Social Life*, New York: Peter Lang, pp. 279–98.

Crisell, Andrew (2012) *Liveness and Recording in the Media*, Basingstoke:
Palgrave Macmillan.

Croft, John (2007) 'Theses on Liveness', *Organised Sound*, 12:1, 59–66.

Darnton, Robert (1984) *The Great Cat Massacre, and Other Episodes in
French Cultural History*, New York: Basic Books.

Department of Culture, Media and Sport (2008) *Encouraging
Digital Access to Culture*. Found at: http://fm.typepad.com/files/
dcms_encouraging_digital_access_to_culture.pdf.

Digital Cinema Initiatives (2005) 'Digital Cinema System Specification'.
Found at: http://www.dcimovies.com/archives/spec_v1/
DCI_Digital_Cinema_System_Spec_v1.pdf.

Digital Cinema Report (2011) 'Digital Cinema's First Decade'. Found at:
http://www.digitalcinemareport.com/node/1431.

Donahue, Anne (2003) 'Techies Give Alternative Programming a
Thumbs-Up', *Variety*, 3 February.

Drake, Philip (2006) 'Reconceptualising Screen Performance', *Journal of
Film and Video*, 58:1–2, 84–94.

Ellis, John (1982) *Visible Fictions*, London: Routledge, Kegan & Paul.

European Digital Cinema Forum (n.d.) 'The EDCF Guide to Alternative
Content in Cinemas'. Found at: http://www.edcf.net/edcf_docs/
edcf_alt_content_for_dcinema.pdf.

European Union (n.d.) 'Draft Communication on
Digitisation of Cinemas'. Found at: http://ec.europa.eu/
culture/media/programme/overview/consultations/docs/
background_digital_cinema_en.pdf.

Feuer, Jane (1983) 'The Concept of Live Television: Ontology as
Ideology', in E. Ann Kaplan (ed.), *Regarding Television*, Los Angeles:
American Film Institute, pp. 12–22.

Fischer-Lichte, Erika (2008) *The Transformative Power of Performance: A
New Aesthetics*, New York: Routledge.

Forde, Leon (2002a) 'Alternative Cinema Content Remains an
Unexploited Revenue Stream', *Screen Daily*, 28 June.

Forde, Leon (2002b) 'Cinema Expo Seminar Poses the $10bn Digital
Question', *Screen Daily*, 1 July.

Friend, Marion (2003) '*Operatunity* Evaluation Report', London: Arts
Council England.

Frith, Simon (2007) 'Live Music Matters', *Scottish Music Review*, 1:1, 1–17.

DOI: 10.1057/9781137288691

Galupo, Scott (2007) 'Beyond the Movie Theater', *Washington Times*, 12 April. Found at: http://www.washingtontimes.com/news/2007/apr/12/20070412-094039-3910r/?page=all.

Garnham, Nicholas (1990) *Capitalism and Communication: Global Culture and the Economics of Information*, London: Sage.

Garnham, Nicholas (2005) 'From Cultural to Creative Industries: An Analysis of the Implications of the "Creative Industries" Approach to Arts and Media Policy Making in the United Kingdom', *International Journal of Cultural Policy*, 11:1, 15–29.

Gilbey, Ryan (2012) 'Banish the Truffle Oil', *New Statesman*, 17 April.

Glévarec, Hervé (2005) 'La Fin du modèle classique de la légitimité culturelle. Hétérogénéisation des ordres de légitimité et régime contemporain de justice culturelle. L'Exemple du champ musical', in Eric Maigret and Eric Macé (eds), *Penser les médiacultures: Nouvelles Pratiques et nouvelles approches de la représentation du monde*, Paris: Armand Colin-INA.

Gomery, Douglas (1985) 'Theater Television: The Missing Link of Technological Change in the US Motion Picture Industry', *Velvet Light Trap*, 21, 54–61.

Gray, Richard (2010) *Cinemas in Britain: A History of Cinema Architecture*, London: Lund Humphries.

Hancock, David (2011) 'Alternative Content in Cinemas', *Screen Digest*, 22 March. Found at: http://www.screendigest.com/reports/2011222a/2011_03_alternative_content_in_cinemas/view.html.

Heyer, Paul (2008) 'Live from the Met: Digital Broadcast Cinema, Medium Theory, and Opera for the Masses', *Canadian Journal of Communication*, 33, 591–604.

Johnson, James H. (1996) *Listening in Paris: A Cultural History*, Berkeley: University of California Press.

Jones, Charlotte and David Hancock (2009) 'Alternative Content in Cinemas: Market Assessment and Forecasts to 2014', *Screen Digest Report*, 27 November.

Keaney, Emily (2008) 'Understanding Arts Audiences: Existing Data and What It Tells Us', *Cultural Trends*, 17:2, 97–113.

Keeping, Melissa (2012) 'AAM Scales Down Alternative Content Division', *Digital Cinema Report*. Found at: http://www.digitalcinemareport.com/AAM-alternative-content.

Keeping, Melissa and Karsten Grummit (2011) *Alternative Content*, London: Dodona Research.

DOI: 10.1057/9781137288691

Kemp, Stuart (2002) 'Exhib Panel Eyes Alternative Fare', *Hollywood Reporter*, 25 June.

Kirkley, Richard Bruce (1990) 'Image and Imagination: The Concept of Electronic Theatre', *Canadian Theatre Review*, 64, 4–12.

Koven, M. J. (2008) *Film, Folklore and Urban Legends*, Lanham, MD: Scarecrow Press.

Kozel, Susan (2008) *Closer: Performance, Technologies, Phenomenology*, Cambridge, MA: MIT Press.

Krämer, Peter (1996) 'The Lure of the Big Picture: Film, Television and Hollywood', in John Hill and Martin McLoone (eds), *Big Picture, Small Screen: The Relations between Film and Television*, Luton: John Libbey Media, pp. 9–46.

Lahire, Bernard (2003) 'From the Habitus to an Individual Heritage of Dispositions: Towards a Sociology at the Level of the Individual', *Poetics*, 31:5–6, 329–55.

Levine, Lawrence (1990) *Highbrow/Lowbrow: The Emergence of Cultural Hierarchy in America*, Cambridge, MA: Harvard University Press.

Lewis, Justin, Stephen Cushion and James Thomas (2005) 'Immediacy, Convenience, or Engagement? An Analysis of 24-Hour News Channels in the UK', *Journalism Studies*, 6:4, 461–77.

Maigret, Eric (2012) 'Bande dessinée et postlégitimité', in Eric Maigret and Matteo Stefanelli (eds), *La Bande dessinée: Une Médiaculture*, Paris, Armand Colin-INA.

Marriott, Stephanie (2007) *Live Television: Time, Space and the Broadcast Event*, London: Sage.

Martindale, Sarah (2011) 'An Investigation of the Status of "Shakespeare", and the Ways in Which This Is Manifested in Audience Responses, with Specific Reference to Three Late-1990s Shakespearean Films', PhD Thesis, Aberystwyth University.

McGloin, Rory, Kirstie M. Farrar and Marina Krcmar (2011) 'The Impact of Controller Naturalness on Spatial Presence, Gamer Enjoyment, and Perceived Realism in a Tennis Simulation Video Game', *Presence*, 20:4, 309–24.

McGregor, Brent (1997) *Live, Direct and Biased? Making Television News in the Satellite Age*, London: Arnold.

Merritt, Rick (2004) 'Soon Movies Will No Longer Be "Films"', *Electronic Engineering Times*, 11 October.

Miller, Nod and Rod Allen (eds) (1993) *It's Live – But Is It Real?* Luton: John Libbey Media.

DOI: 10.1057/9781137288691

Monaco, James (1997) *How to Read a Film: Technology, Language, History and Theory of Film and Media*, New York: Oxford University Press.

Moran, Nick (2010) 'Resisting the Lure of the Screen', *International Journal of Performance Arts and Digital Media*, June, 77–88.

Narval Media/Birkbeck College/Media Consulting Group (2009) *Stories We Tell Ourselves: The Cultural Impact of UK Film, 1946–2006*, report to the UK Film Council. Found at: http://industry.bfi.org.uk/media/pdf/f/i/CIReport_010709.pdf.

Nelson, Philip (1970) 'Information and Consumer Behavior', *Journal of Political Economy*, 78, 311–29.

NESTA (2004) 'Annual Report'. Found at: http://www.nesta.org.uk/library/documents/2004_2005_Annual_Report.pdf.

NESTA (2010) 'Beyond Live: Digital Innovation in the Performing Arts'. Found at: http://www.nesta.org.uk/about_us/assets/features/beyond_live.

New Economics Foundation (2011) *Capturing the Audience Experience: A Handbook for the Theatre*, London: New Economics Foundation. Found at: http://www.itc-arts.org/uploaded/documents/Theatre%20handbook.pdf.

Northern Alliance and Ipsos MediaCT (2011) *Opening Our Eyes: How Film Contributes to the Culture of the UK*, London: BFI.

NT Live (2010) 'Digital Broadcast of Theatre: Learning from the Pilot Season'. Found at: http://www.nesta.org.uk/library/documents/NTLive_web.pdf.

O'Brien, Dave (2010) *Measuring the Value of Culture: A Report to the Department of Culture, Media and Sport*. Found at: http://www.culture.gov.uk/images/publications/measuring-the-value-culture-report.pdf.

O'Reilly, Daragh and Finola Kerrigan (eds) (2012) *Marketing the Arts: A Fresh Approach*, London: Routledge.

Ostrower, Francis (2005) *Motivations Matter: Findings and Practical Implications of a National Survey on Cultural Participation*, Washington DC: Urban Institute.

Oxford Economics (2007) *The Economic Impact of the UK Film Industry*, report to the UK Film Council. Found at: http://industry.bfi.org.uk/media/pdf/5/8/FilmCouncilreport190707.pdf.

Palmer, Daniel (2010) 'Webcams: The Aesthetics of Liveness', *LIKE: Art Magazine*, 12, 16–22.

Petley, Julian (2011) *Film and Video Censorship in Modern Britain*, Edinburgh: Edinburgh University Press.

DOI: 10.1057/9781137288691

Peterson, Richard A. and Roger M. Kern (1996) 'Changing Highbrow Taste: From Snob to Omnivore', *American Sociological Review*, 61:5, 900–7.

Phelan, Peggy (1993) *Unmarked: The Politics of Performance*, London: Routledge.

Poynor, Rick (2001) *Obey the Giant: Life in the Image World*, Berlin: Birkhäuser.

PR Newswire (2005) 'Access Integrated Technologies Digitally Delivers Morrissey Concert to Ten Movie Screens throughout the U.S.', *PR Newswire*, 29 March.

Putnam, Robert (2000) *Bowling Alone: The Collapse and Revival of American Community*, New York: Simon & Schuster.

Radbourne, Jennifer, Hilary Glow and Katya Johanson (2010) 'Measuring the Intrinsic Benefits of Arts Attendance', *Cultural Trends*, 19:4, 307–24.

Reason, Matthew (2006) *Documentation, Disappearance and the Representation of Live Performance*, Basingstoke: Palgrave Macmillan.

Regenbrecht, Holger T., Elizabeth A. Franz, Graham McGregor, Brian G. Dixon and Simon Hoermann (2011) 'Beyond the Looking Glass: Fooling the Brain with the Augmented Mirror Box', *Presence*, 20:6, 559–76.

Robinson, Piers (2002) *The CNN Effect: The Myth of News, Foreign Policy and Intervention*, London: Routledge.

Rumbold, Kate (2008) 'The Arts Council England's "Arts Debate"', *Cultural Trends*, 17:3, 189–95.

Rutter, Jason (1997) 'Stand-Up as Interaction: Performance and Audience in Comedy Venues', PhD Thesis, University of Salford.

Santana, Ivani and Fernando Iazzetta (n.d.) 'Liveness in Mediatized Dance Performance – An Evolutionary and Semiotic Perspective'. Found at: http://www.eca.usp.br/prof/iazzetta/papers/santana_iazzetta.pdf.

Scannell, Paddy (2012) *Television and the Meaning of 'Live'*, Cambridge: Polity.

Scarpetta, Fabiola and Anna Spagnolli (2009) 'The Interactional Context of Humour in Stand-Up Comedy', *Research on Language and Social Interaction*, 42:3, 210–30.

Shafer, Daniel M., Corey P. Carbonara and Lucy Popova (2011) 'Spatial Presence and Perceived Reality as Predictors of Motion-Based Video Game Enjoyment', *Presence*, 20:6, 591–619.

DOI: 10.1057/9781137288691

Sheppard, Anthony (2007) 'Review of the Metropolitan Opera's New HD Movie Theater Broadcasts', *American Music*, 25:3, 383–7.

Shin, Dong-Hee and Youn-Joo Shin (2011) 'Consumers' Trust in Virtual Mall Shopping: The Role of Social Presence and Perceived Security', *International Journal of Human–Computer Interaction*, 27:5, 450–75.

Silpayamanant, Jon (2011) 'The Death of the Cinematic Industry'. Found at: http://silpayamanant.wordpress.com/tag/livecast/.

Stam, Robert and Alessandra Raengo (eds) (2004a) *A Companion to Literature and Film*, New York: Wiley.

Stam, Robert and Alessandra Raengo (2004b) *Literature and Film: A Guide to the Theory and Practice of Film Adaptation*, New York: Wiley.

Stewart, Andrew (2010) '3D's Diminishing Box Office Returns', *Variety*, 22 June.

Storey, John (2010) *Culture and Power in Cultural Studies: The Politics of Signification*, Edinburgh: Edinburgh University Press.

Tambling, Jeremy (1987) *Opera, Ideology and Film*, New York: St. Martin's Press.

Trueman, Matt (2009) 'Is the Live Theatre Experience Dying?', *Guardian*, 19 October.

UPI (2007a) 'Metropolitan Opera Woos Younger Fans', news release, 26 April.

UPI (2007b) 'Domingo's Voice Fills U.S. Movie Theaters', news release, 14 January.

Urry, John (2002) 'Mobility and Proximity', *Sociology*, 36:2, 255–74.

van Uffelen, Chris (2009) *Cinema Architecture*, Switzerland: Braun.

Vianello, Robert (1985) 'The Power "Politics" of Live Television', *Journal of Film & Video*, 37:3, 26–40.

Walker, Chris and Stephanie Scott-Melnyk, with Kay Sherwood (2002) *Reggae to Rachmaninoff: How and Why People Participate in Arts and Culture*, Washington DC: Urban Institute.

Weed, Mike (2007) 'The Pub as a Virtual Football Fandom Venue: An Alternative to "Being There"?', *Soccer and Society*, 8:2, 399–414.

Weed, Mike (2010) 'Sport Fans and Travel – Is "Being There" Always Important?', *Journal of Sport and Tourism*, 15:2, 103–9.

Whannel, Garry and John Horne (2008) 'Beer Sponsors Football: What Could Go Wrong?', in Lawrence A. Wenner and Steven J. Jackson (eds), *Sport, Beer, and Gender: Promotional Culture & Contemporary Social Life*, New York: Peter Lang, pp. 55–74.

DOI: 10.1057/9781137288691

Williams, Linda (1999) *Hardcore: Power, Pleasure and the 'Frenzy of the Visible'*, Berkeley: University of California Press.

Woods, Penelope (2007) 'Globe Audiences: Spectatorship and Reconstruction at Shakespeare's Globe', PhD Thesis, Queen Mary, University of London.

Woolfe, Zachary (2012) 'I'm Ready for My Close-Up, Mr Puccini', *New York Times*, 27 April.

Ytreberg, Espen (2006) 'Premeditations of Performance in Recent Live Television: A Scripting Approach to Media Production Studies', *European Journal of Cultural Studies*, 9:4, 421–40.

DOI: 10.1057/9781137288691

Index

DOI: 10.1057/9781137288691

DOI: 10.1057/9781137288691

DOI: 10.1057/9781137288691

CPSIA information can be obtained at www.ICGtesting.com
Printed in the USA
LVOW08*1431160514

386132LV00006B/81/P

Rec June 2014

Date Due
